New Selected Poems

Geoff Page

PUNCHER & WATTMANN

First published in 2013
Published by Puncher and Wattmann
PO Box 441
Glebe NSW 2037
http://www.puncherandwattmann.com
puncherandwattmann@bigpond.com

National Library of Australia
Cataloguing-in-Publication entry:

Page, Geoff
New Selected Poems

ISBN   9781922186454

I. Title.

A821.3
Cover design by Matthew Holt

Printed by McPhersons Printing Group

This project has been assisted by the
Australian Government through the
Australia Council, its arts funding and
advisory body.

Australian Government

Australia Council
for the Arts

Contents

from Clairvoyant in Autumn (1983)

Road Show

At the end of his act
the softshoe possum
the spotlights hard
upon him,
> danced

one step and made
a final bow.
The Holden, however,
not brought up
to vaudeville,
swept on,
> printing

the bitumen with
a whiskery gesture.

Jazz/Poet

he scrawled
a sudden
sentence in
the air

violent yet
articulate

I snatched
a phrase

and took
it home
to work on

but
by dawn

it was
dead

For William Carlos Williams

As with
the newborn
of Rutherford

you took
life's drifting scraps
by the feet

with worn hands
slapped them
into breath

and smiled
to hear them bawl
so wisely.

Wartime Memory

They came
strung out
one windy morning
Wirraways,
seven or eight of them,
banking in file
around the downstream bend.
I stood
on a bluff
outside our house
and watched
them pass

so close
I saw where
brown met green
and helmet-heads
turned stiffly
in the perspex.
The sound swung
through the valley,
jarred the inert pools.

Then the upstream turn;
to leave an echo dying,
and me, just five,
still gazing —
at an empty river bend.

Back-road Churches

Out on back-roads
the churches are dying.
The priest drives back
across his sixty
years less often.
Yards of dusty
Fords thin out;
and men's stiff suits,
their wives' uncertain
hats, grow rare
across the grass.

Saturday night,
a bottle through
a window. Shadows
reel in lantern
light, thrusting
thighs of charcoal
nudes up hard
against the wall.
Afterwards, even
the timbers are spread
to the wind's need.
The night is measured
by a banging door.

Out there, adrift
on distant ridges,
the churches strain
beneath the wind.

Country Nun

In a café under a lazy fan
she talks with her brother,
the breath of cows upon him,
a line of sun and hat across his brow.
Wimpled above the steak and peas,

she drifts away / drifts back,
floating as she did
in cowfields of their childhood,
lingering on the few books in the living room,
always last to the pool.

From rough-sawn walls
beyond the memory of decision
she moves through knee-high pastures
to a convent gate
farewell.

Soon now
he will need to walk her back,
feeling her lift already
towards the pure insistence
of the bell.

Bert

Now, as then,
on homestead backsteps,
taking his orders for the day ...
      pale, disquieted eyes and sweated hat
      at the wrong end of a lifetime
      with someone else's cattle.

Far back, when the boss
was fresh from the city,
and both were young,
Bert showed him, as
a kind of friend,
the vagaries of fences and old cows ...
      mustering down spurs
      towards the yards,
      riding home tired horses
      by the river.

But somehow
the run of weather, the cattle generations
have spent them differently.
The boss, grey now but safe
with heirs and acres, finds
for Bert's sprained heart each morning

a closer paddock:
        tall sons take saddle early
        for the mountains.

And Bert rides out each day
on orders
towards a town parkbench,
        a fine gratuity
        of pigeons.

Smalltown Memorials

No matter how small
Every town has one;
Maybe just the obelisk,
A few names inlaid;
More often full-scale granite,
Marble digger (arms reversed),
Long descending lists of dead.
Sometimes not even a town,
A thickening of houses
Or a few unlikely trees
Glimpsed on a back-road
Will have one.

1919, 1920:
All over the country;
Maybe a band, slow march;
Mayors, shire councils;
Relatives for whom
Print was already
Only print; mates,
Come back, moving
Into unexpected days;
A ring of Fords and sulkies;
The toned-down bit
Of Billy Hughes from an
Ex-recruiting sergeant.
Unveiled;
Then seen each day —
Noticed once a year;

And then not always,
Everywhere.

The next bequeathed us
Parks and pools
But something in that first
Demanded stone.

Bondi Afternoon 1915

Elioth Gruner

The wind plays through
the painted weather.

No cloud. The sea
and air, one blue.

A hemisphere
away from gunfire

an artist finds
his image for the year:

a girl in white
blown muslin, walking

in the last
clear afternoon.

Christ at Gallipoli

This synod is convinced that the forces
of the Allies are being used of God to
vindicate the rights of the weak and to
maintain the moral order of the world.

Anglican Synod, Melbourne, 1916.

Bit weird at first,
That starey look in the eyes,
The hair down past his shoulders,
But after a go with the ship's barber,
A sea-water shower and the old slouch hat
Across his ears, he started to look the part.
Took him a while to get the way
A bayonet fits the old Lee-Enfield,
But going in on the boats
He looked calmer than any of us,
Just gazing in over the swell
Where the cliffs looked black against the sky.
When we hit he fairly raced in through the waves,
Then up the beach, swerving like a full-back at the end
When the Turks'd really got on to us.
Time we all caught up,
He was off like a flash, up the cliffs,
After his first machine gun.
He'd done for three Turks when we got there,
The fourth was a gibbering mess.
Seeing him wave that blood-red bayonet,
I reckoned we were glad
To have him on the side.

Bowls

From sixty-five
to the last dark family gathering
they walk rolled turf
up down all week from end to end,
the slow bowls arching out
then in towards the jack.
Thinned out but undismayed
by strokes and skipping hearts
they stroll up down together
in the crisp white reassurance
of their clothes, miles each week,
replenished inexhaustibly by more
fresh out from short farewells
and thanks engraved in plate.
On a road beyond the hedge
the world unreasonably runs on;
children call in, turning grey;
caravans in winter sway
north behind the sun;
but here on close-trimmed turf
the frayed dispersing ends of life
are knit — then rolled
with slow control
towards the jack.

Saturday Night

saturday night
just after 12

a whiff of sex
in the air

couples' cars
slide home up drives

clipped gardens
wait
between two days

fat girls
are whisked
off home through mist

& the suburb begins
to make love

pairs at first
then unison

houses streets
& gardens
the whole suburb

rocking in undulations
towards

one long collective
cry

then sleep

outside the gardens
recollect themselves

& wait it out
till dawn

Far End

1.
Sixty-five
by the time I knew her
nipping along
in lean black
dresses and flat
determined hats
skirmishing out
to jackhammer mornings
trams and concrete
checking the scales
watching the decades
hitch their skirts
hurrying back
to the bachelor son
home from the war
and home from the bank
at seven.

2.
He died at fifty.
She came north to the next
but he too like the first
and so to the daughter

lost these thirty years
to cattle country
where wind
streamed all the day
through stiff grey trees
and even an afternoon
of streets
was forty miles
beyond a possibility.
Now
no longer checking
births and deaths
she circles thinly
at the edges of the family
as it strides down
undeflected
on its money.

Wrinkles draw in
across fine bone
towards the mouth.

She enters her ninetieth year.

3.
On a visit this time
(a new spring morning)
I sit with her
and watch her stringing beans
the first ones done
ten years
inside another century.

I start to talk
of a house she knows
(and I have seen) is now
a patch of rubbled earth:
the tiled front steps
go upward into nothing.
Between us
we put back the details:
ferns in the hall
the stained-glass door
old clocks, lost books
the long dark easy spaces.
'A lovely old home,' she says
three times
in as many minutes
her mind winding
in a sad caprice
past faded aunts
and menfolk with
exhausted hearts
back to a bulldozed house.

I see now
in this spring sun
stringing beans
at the far end of all her
containment
she is crying.

Love at the End

Forty years ... our bodies quiet,
thin sheets an easy load for spindle bones,

a window pales towards dawn and the general
catastrophe seeping in over the skyline.

So, in a private end of night, we listen
for the light capricious flicker of our hearts,

hollow and dry, like ping-pong balls, clicking
towards and then away from unison.

Fingers linked, we float towards that last
stopped moment when one will hand the other through

alone
to disbelief   and silence.

End of the Season

Further up
We found the lift
Had just tied off the winter.
Snow held in dirty patches:
The sky was clean.
At the chalet
It had gone completely.
A wind pushed up
And over the granite scarp,
Testing dry spaces of weatherboard,
The sun-warped green of sills and stairs.
Peering from the verandah
We saw in a drawing room, perhaps
The last two guests at 'Chopsticks',
A businessman in the corner.
Outside, under glass, a huge map
Of all the Victorian railways —
Nothing else shown.

The wind, half-lost in dusty trees,
The wind, maybe the weatherboard,
Brings something back —
My parents' honeymoon.
They only talked of it once:
The high log fire, the long framed
View of the valley,
The inevitable and accomplished
Girl at the piano.

And outside, thinning
Off into October,
The final snow
Of 1939.

Hóra Sfakíon

First retsina of the day
enveloped by a blue of sea and sky
so clear two fishing boats
are moored in air —

a dome of glass
and meditation
broken by a kid
that goes past upside down
leg-roped
and bleating with foreknowledge.
When wine and summer noon
are shimmering in the brain
the man comes back
the small stilled meat
on a hook.

On the headland
in an afternoon
of wind and resinous pine
there is a sudden cross
to partisans
beneath it, a small window
yellow with skulls.

Evening returns us
to tables and chairs:
the sea and sky
drain slowly to one colour.

Walking to Kritsa

Farming dust between
wind & granite she is a
blowing tent of grief

     *

The sky is turning
A donkey hauls a woman
& a sled — steel on
stone to free the grain —
wheeling all one day's
circumference of yellow

     *

Cool water down from
rocks & sky climbs slowly back
the stems of lemons

     *

& now the first old
men in doorways   goat bells in
the vanished weather

The Catacomb

is a liner settling,
its plates askew
with martyrs and all
the stars gone out.
Deep under sea
in the long free-fall
there is throughout
the hope of uplift
the knowledge
of drowning,
a dreaming of rescue
and the steady
descent. From the moment
of impact
the liner will be
a cathedral of
iron forever.

Inscription at Villers-Bretonneux

The dead at Villers-Bretonneux
rise gently on a slope towards
the sky. The land is trim — skylines

of ploughed earth and steeples; unfallen
rain still hanging in the air;
confusion smoothed away

and everything put back — the village
too   (red brick/white sills)   in nineteen
twenty, unchanged since. Headstones

speak a dry consensus. Just one
breaks free: 'Lives Lost, Hearts Broken —
And for What?' I think of the woman

and those she saddened by insisting —
the Melbourne clerk
who must have let it through.

Coloratura

The groans of love
at 3 a.m.
A rickety hotel

spindled on
a spine of stairs
a block from the Boul' Mich.

Italian maybe,
she moans towards climax
and holds us fixed

next door
involuntary voyeurs.

A fleshy prima donna
in her prime
each breast a handful

the lifted thighs
her straight-man
in between

bringing her to it
five or six times
before dawn.

Champagne and wireless
in occasional spaces
her voice only.

A half hour
illusion of sleep
and then again

the throaty cry
soaring to coloratura.

Stiffly we lie
in cold damp sheets
and listen.

So much, so little space
between two faces
of a wall.

Somewhere between 4 a.m. & 6

One will wake
beside another & lying still
will feel the outlines of the room suspended

awaiting light,
will feel the spaced pale
cries of birds as night fails

into dawn & away at the edge of hearing
a car will accelerate & vanish, a misting
rain just damp enough to slick

the road. Despair should be a trick
of light — the ceiling
for an hour will offer nothing.

Life leaks away
& houses joined by drifting rain
are held until a ratchet point is reached ...

A scatter of clocks
revives the lie
that all may not be lost.

Unsolved Crime

In the city of curves and carpeted space
the veneer will for an instant warp
to let a body through;
some strange divergence building to a clot
spills and is gone,
the car with its bootload headed outwards.
The streetfront doors are steadily opaque;
a hand hangs over the phone forever.
A wandering boy and then police
discover what's left by time and the weather —
and each lead checks off into air.
The family take hands for a last translation
to smoke and ash. A newspaper's
slight remembrance fails. And somewhere
out on the easy curves
someone is driving twice a day
with images — the case now filed away
in steel, the nervous typescript hanging sideways
— driving every day alone
with images that swerve and scar
even as they vanish.

Ideal Couple

By counterpoint
they speak one mind

the makeshift world
no longer tempts them

and two who grow
from such a bond

are blonde and full of promise.
Life it seems

is a workable substance
shaped by the steady will

plans drawn up
proceed to their fulfilment.

Strange whispers of the skin
if they occur will draw them inwards

never split the seal.
Meeting them at parties

couples from the outer world
and slightly broken by it

will see them as a measure
of their failure

and driving home
be no less happy

under the uncertain stars.

Black Wind

A black wind
from the southern ocean
tests the grip
of spinifex on
shifting soil.
Road & rail
hold straight
for eighty miles,
cross twice.
Lights flow
either way, collide
then burst apart.
A night express
howls down
stretched wire
between two cities.
The wind
lifts once

then flows
towards the centre.

The Photographs

The photographs
arrive long-distance —
the seal pup staring

up at the club
stopped in the snap
of a shutter, the whale

harpooned with its brain
exploding winched
to the flensing knives.

We would forget
how we surfaced from time
and will be returning

down through a legend
to a valley of rain
and the widening water.

Do not be grieved,
we would say to the whale
in a ghostly sonar,

we also are bound
for a harbour of blood.

Not Yet

Somehow the shape
of the game has broken.
High in the village
of thinning air
three aldermen are at a
table in the square
shaded by their dry
complaining. Workmen
dressed in cooling sweat
go by without a glance.
The lean men of the future
are working back elsewhere
while in a club set high
to catch the clouds
a few old names have almost
blown away. The evening
has not yet brought
the rumours from the border.
The lean men bent
beneath their lamps
work down their lists and figures
rehearsing the word
Necessity — not yet
to each other.

Aubade

Roosters perched at the town's far edge
lift from high fences
the light out of darkness

to fill our rented window
then let its space be used
by other sound:

a plane tree quickening with starlings
the magpie's song of cold wind in the sun
and lastly the Sunday bell

buffeting still air.
At each stroke comes
some clarity of childhood

our own or others further still
days of eucalypt and horse sweat
days of the donkey and lemon grove.

Turning in our tumbled blankets
with last night's love
remembered on the skin

we listen to the world
fill up with light
and with our losses.

Last Draft

You're wondering why my light's still on — twenty-
Four years straight, twenty again before that —
Why should I write when you sleep right down the hall?
Why not say it? You know that's not our way.
Ours is the way of silence, the whole day strung
To signs: the quiet nod over morning eggs,
A table set the night before, the quick
Goodbye on bright front steps, alternating
Grills/baked meats, the changing of channels from grey
To grey. Why take the pen when I could say it?
Not just the sheer unlikelihood of ever
Really speaking, but also via such cross-outs
And deletions I may myself begin
To understand. You know I love you — whatever
That may mean. That may be what they say
In shops, seeing us together, what those
Who know may think, seeing me with mop
And bucket now your bones turn brittle. Outside
These walls you're the absolute old lady, white-haired,
Kind, a lovely piece of porcelain
Fragility — and so you are to me,
A little worn with what might seem a close
Acquaintance but why else am I here at fifty?
Did you one day think I could have wished
For something different: a home hung white with napkins
On a winter afternoon, a floorful of
Toys to trip up on, a flat of my own to try
Remaindered women, a place to sit up late
With friends? Don't think, Mother, I don't know how

You organise your mind — T's too shy,
Too broken by the war; four bleak years
In Stalag 17, too late to try
Uncharted waters now; better moored
And let the currents roll on up the coast
Than risk the tricky tides of others' love.
Besides, I hear you stop yourself from thinking,
What about me? A house should have a man.
Father gave up early; there was a space
To fill; I came back from the war; the job
Was mine. Twenty-five years of slowly freezing
Over. At first I used to think of them —
typists in daydreams, easing their legs apart;
Even at times the more fantastic step
Of signing names in cheap hotels downtown.
(I'm sorry, Mother, I'll drop this bit next draft.
This warm indecent talk is in poor taste
Although, like every widow's son, I conjure
How, unthinkably, you must have moved
Between the sheets so many years ago.)
Enough of that. The point is, Mother, I cannot
Bear the shape of disappointment in
Your eyes. Escape hangs off the margin. My gaze
Goes to the wardrobe top, the case with its troopship
Tag. But walking with it down the hall
And past your ferns in early morning light ...
You would not even need to break your sleep.
But to be fair, I know you could be right.
I live by ritual, by channels and
Procedures: the bus trip either way, the evening
Television (what did we do before that?),
The bachelor bed, its fine singularity.

Clubs and dinner invitations (if
They came) could only jolt routine. In fact,
We feed each other — the gift of ritual.
But, to return. There is a widow at
The office now who dreams of something human
In me still. So far, smiles and politeness
Only, of course, but somehow she lets me know
It might ... Not greatly given to fantasy
(As you know), I try to see her in
This house (Aunt Ada's room?) then contemplate
My suitcase, the impossible walk down the hall. Don't worry
Too much, Mother, I wouldn't call it love —
Just a glimpsed horizon. As for sex,
That seems so brief and so far back I'd have
To learn again. Her warmth is more in spirit
Than the loins. Her smile's the thing. I know
You're still awake down there, watching this late
Reflected light fill up the glass above
Your door. Four nights now — and yet no question.
We ritualists are strong on privacy.
I'll check this just once more for truth; then stow
It in my drawer. One morning soon, I swear it,
Mother, you'll find out why this light burns late;
You'll find just once the breakfast call unanswered,
These two neat sheets of paper on your plate.

At 95

Coming to say goodbye
— what else at 95?
we find you gone already,
a ghost in outer rooms.
Two jobs they leave you
to moor you to the world.
Stringing beans and ironing
and in the long retreats
that pass for sleep
you find again the exact shade
of a skirting board,
scratched patterns on a door,
that grainy air, long afternoons
of rubbing silver, sharp words
of a stepsister — not easily forgiven …
Full-time work, this
dusty midwest 1880's girlhood …
and sometimes you smile back
as through a half-closed door
but it's too late.
We're using now
that loudness meant
for foreigners and children;
and as we leave you ask three times
do we have a car.

Detail

She waits at the window.
A light breeze &
a traffic smear.

From the view he had
when he was 8
& trains blew clouds

his grandmother (92)
is watching also
the railway yard.

The sill traps
a shudder of diesel —
the house is now a Home.

He comes
somehow to thank her
for white streets

of a childhood.
She looks from the window;
speaks just once ...

of the woman
beached
in the bed behind her

both legs
cut off at the thigh.
He looks around.

Two red coals
in a crumpled face
insist

that legs still stride
from kitchen to copper
& spread each year

for children.
The silence comes again.
Grandmother & grandson.

The years are
turning transparent.
The window frames

a last half-hour,
the unbreakable logic
of trains.

Detail in a War Museum

Behind a door that reads STAFF ONLY
there is a corridor of them,
mannequins unclothed and leaning

awkwardly along a wall.
Jaws set square, hair trimmed to sail
eyes sky-blue with resolution

it seems they're almost ready now
wanting only fresh khaki
some slight adjustment of the limbs

and lastly orders — which war to
go back to? which war yet to come?

Brothers

Two days beyond the Last Post dawn
The khaki streets and brass at ten
These plastic wreaths survive,
Apex, Lions and Rotary, courtesy the florist —
Also a bunch of dahlias
Dilute-yellow and a shoebox card
Filled carefully in biro.

In loving memory of my brothers
Pte. K.L. McK---, Lone Pine 1915
Pte. T.K. McK---, France 1917
Pte. P.L. McK---, France 1918
                    Gnr. S.L. McK, 1st A.I.F.

Old man in a kitchen. 4 a.m.
One bare bulb above his head.
Scissors, string, a mug with steam
And flowers dew-wet across the table.
He finds the words again.

And somewhere just beyond them still
Four boys run in a steel-grey paddock
Headlong for the wire.

Trench Dreams

... of Paris as it will be when we rise
short-breathed from three years' mud
to boulevards that hang clairvoyant

in afternoons of impossible air
when troopships have departed south
with slouch hats & a scattered song

& jazz tunes ring the first Americans
when cafés fill with smoke & four years' conversation
& whores move on the streets like hefty flowers ...

     A whistle swings us
     over the top
     to falter at last on gunfire

     & trench dreams float face-down
     as heirlooms, aching
     at the edge of sleep.

Home Front

After the morning in Martin Place
with sidestepping faces and a clutch of white feathers
her tram sways home past harbour street-ends
uneasy with so much conviction.

The afternoon is given to verses:
tomorrow, socks. Nouns are flags
heroically abstract and verbs
are tight with rightful anger

and she will speak of the Somme
as *a river of pure love*
a river from which perhaps
right now a telegram with name attached

will shatter her resolve forever
or make it iron with grief.

Harney

So when I got back to Australia
I got off at Melbourne
and went straight through
back to the north with horses
the skylines passing beneath me
a slow kind of forgiveness.
Why didn't you go to the war?
they'd say as I asked for some tucker
and I'd say *that's my business*
remembering from so much killing

       a regimental band
       and all its instruments
       dismembered by a shell,
       three German prisoners
       stumbling back to English lines
       with one hand to salute between them ...

Memorials if they have to
I can just understand;
speeches though I never went for —
waistcoats and watchchains
the phrases come easy.
A talker myself in a way
I came at length to books
and left the war as it should have been —
decently unwritten.

Letters

The top of their heads
were blown off with machine guns.
It was a horrible sight.
Blood and brains

had trickled down the faces
and dried. I was filled with delight
to see so many Huns killed and could not
help laughing ...

Not poetry exactly
our letters lie
in cupboards later
tied with a dusty ribbon.

We were the one in four
who never made the boat.
Tomorrow's death gave clarity
no school could ever give.

We have to go back again
thats the crook Part about,
once I used to be able
to look at dead and shattered men

and crook sights,
without turning a hair,
there were a few thousand at 'Lone Pine'
but now I get nervy.

Been at it too long
without a spell I think.

Our photographs are curled up now
thrown out
with the homes that kept them —
the ones on file are no less lost.

In cupboards or forgotten drawers
and tied with a dusty ribbon
our words converge without intent
upon a single point.

Burial in Air

In town on a cedar shelf
his last commands
are folded lengthwise.

Already in the night
he knows himself as ashes.
Beyond the furnace door
the shadows of his bones

are broken,
shaken out to a copper urn
and from the slipstream of a plane
launched into the wind

dry rain
across his land: the ironbark
cattle camps on ridges,
the sodden shining gullies.

The river at night
holds a single note
and curves into the sky.

Cassandra Paddocks

He was a reader, the great-niece says
waving a hand over tea and scones
cancelling a dozen outer paddocks
and bringing out like heirloom silver
components of a life between the lines:
the delicate mother who insisted
on Oxford for the eldest — and lost
the rest before the age of two;
the classical Tripos — the governess
began it ... a smattering of myth,
nothing much else on these upper reaches,
curly-haired gods the only suitors
and a classical slant to the gums.
After the young sea voyage, quiet towers,
leather shelves and well-honed conversation
he rode the paddocks differently
and left things to a string of overseers.
Stockmen held back from the distance
in his eyes, different, even deeper, than their own.
Named the paddocks Cassandra, Agamemnon,
the great-niece recalls with a laugh;
made all the wrong decisions —
instead of cattle, sheep (which went
to tallow and would not wait for wool).
But books were different.
Had them sent by the crate-load,
clipper, coastal steamer, a final

team of bullocks; the ritual
delving from straw; then open to the nose,
inhaling — a draught of laudanum.
As cedar shelves filled tight
a rim of paddocks fell to neighbours;
the perimeter tightened on the homestead
where slewing gutters and flaky paint
waited a better season.
Wresting himself from leathered air
he'd sometimes take a horse, ruminate
sales, inspect diminishing outposts,
peopling as he rode, fern gullies
with dryads and bacchantes, hearing
in a sudden rush of hooves the flight
of centaurs and in the whipbird's call
the opening note of Pan.
Ambling beside a swayback fence
he'd dream instead down his agent's list —
one book implied at least another two.
Odd trips down to Sydney to the Club
brought in the usual disappointments —
the climate, it seemed, engendered only
saleyard talk and backroom manoeuvre in railways.
Could've lost the lot, you know,
only he died first. His descendant takes
more from the uncle, riding up
after the telegram to set things straight
and hold the borders, the man who stalks
through an absence of maids
to the only real room in the house

and stops, unsettled by something
he'd never wish words to,
a wavering — in the lotus scent of leather,
before the old imperatives
could break in again to save him.

Departure and Return

for my father

1.

You rode the boundaries
of my childhood — days shaped
to the gait of horses, nights
to a filament lamp —
and fended off the bank
another month. There was no time.
Awkwardly you too
would have held me in your arms
feeling the newborn future
waver and stretch out.

2.

At twelve I was gone
to that frosty school
the division already begun.
I held the reins okay
but the cattle milling
through my eyes were all the same
my nights were free
of leaning fences.
Marooned up there in cold blue weather
my mother sent parcels
you the cheques —
and each year found me further out.
Sale days in vacations
you'd show me still
just how a vealer's back should be

explaining me each time around
to stockmen, buyers, auctioneers.
In branding yards or tossing hay
you'd be impressed almost —
and when at last I'd left completely
my brothers filled with one step sideways
a gap they'd hardly seen.

3.

Feeling for the fact below the dream
you read what I have salvaged from such days
your eye for verse like mine for fences
not entirely wrong.
In those few hours in every second year
when I still have the long
road south in my ear
we are talking at angles
as if on some back-road
I'd asked for direction.
The brothers beside me
who grew into your debts and weather
do not need the words I lack —
and yet I've not gone far ...
diverging in the outer fact
continuing the spirit.

4.

All this I know was part of all
my strangeness and affection
this morning as I held newborn
my own son in my arms.

Grit

A doxology

I praise the country women
of my mother's generation
who bred, brought up and boasted
six Australians each —
the nearest doctor fifty miles
on a road cut off by flood;
the women who by wordless men
were courted away from typewriters
and taught themselves to drive —
I praise their style
in the gravel corners.
I praise the snakes they broke in two
and the switch of wire they kept in a cupboard.
I praise what they keep and what they lose —
the long road in to the abattoirs,
the stare which cures
a stockman of shooting swans.
I praise the prints, the wide straw brims
they wore out to the clothes line;
I praise each oily crow that watched them.
I praise the tilting weather —
the dry creeks and the steady floods
and the few good weeks between.
I praise each column in the ledger
they kept up late by mosquito and lamp-light;
the temerity of the banker
reining them in at last — or trying;
the machinations for chequered paddocks

56

swung on the children's names;
the companies just one step ahead;
the tax clerk, in his way, also.
I praise each one of their six children
discovering in turn
the river in its tempers
the rapids and the river trees;
the children who grew up to horse sweat
and those who made it to the city.
I praise the stringy maxims
that served instead of prayers;
also the day that each child found
a slogan not enough,
surprising themselves in a camera flash
and bringing no extra paddocks.
I praise the boast of country women:
they could have been a wife
to any of a dozen men
and damn well made it work.
I praise what I have seen
to be much more than this.
I praise their politics of leather;
the ideologies in a line of cattle;
the minds that would not
stoop to whisky.
I praise their scorn
for the city of options, the scholars
in their turning chairs and air-conditioned theories.
I praise also that moment
when they headed off in tears —
the car in a toolshed failing to start,
a bootful of fencing wire.

I praise the forty years
when they did not. I praise
each day and evening of their lives —
that hard abundance year by year
mapped in a single word.

Prologue

Heading west
and home upriver
into the smoke
from a grassfire spring

I'm slanting up into
the smouldering sun;
reaches of haze
and a colder blue

flicker in the turns.
To the right for a moment
an acre with saplings,
headstones in the

weakening light;
to the left down there
slow cattle on
the sifted flats

the river 'where all
the Royal Navy
might comfortably
ride at anchor'

the waters which closed
on J. L. Michael
the Settlement's
second solicitor

a wound to the temple
'deeply incised'
his death this afternoon
a century and more

behind me
unsolved and brittle
on rusting paper.
Bitumen

gives way to gravel,
grit on the leaves
and on the teeth,
a last sun

on the stony ridges.
The river lifts and slips away
to rapids linked
by sheets of sky

the silences of
perch and mullet.
Trees lean closer
on the turns.

Fire and Water
Earth and Air.
I vanish westward
into smoke.

Morning of the Wreckers

My grandmother's house
in Bondi Junction
the morning of the wreckers ...
A grey light fills
the stained-glass door;
in the pantry there are still
some bottles,
a few Reader's Digests
piled in a corner.
Three clocks are keeping time
elsewhere. The borders
of the garden
forget their definition.
A foreman, drawing up outside,
checks details on a clipboard.
Someone is scrambling
on the roof; the slate tile seems
a concentration of the sky.
In half an hour their dozer
will cough down backwards
off a truck and mount
the tiled front steps,
exploding them to rubble.
Blade upraised
as if against a blow,
one steady rush
will knock the front wall sideways
and bring the roof down
to its knees. Light

gets down between the bricks,
first time for a
hundred years.
A few more slaps
will settle all resistance.
It'll be just a matter
of scraping and lifting
a front-end loader
filling up trucks
that haul away into the traffic.
Three workmen lunch
on a bathroom floor
which also by half past four
will vanish.
By the second day's end
the block will be scoured —
except for a brown
front page of a *Herald*,
a final iris or agapanthus
surviving the swift
crosshatching of metal.
My grandmother's house ...
is a gravel scar
obscured by roofing iron
which reads:

               CBJ Investments

At my grandmother's house
in Bondi Junction
the wreckers
            do not arrive.

White Meat

Ten maybe
I'm scalding a hen
a white leghorn
near the orange tree.

The bucket steams
with watery blood
and the first close smell
of wetted feathers

prelude to the yellow
perfumes of the gut.
The sheets
spread out beside me

remember local teams
and Menzies' second term
then twist to singe
transparent hairs.

White feathers fill
towards a smell
as sour as burning plastic.
Earlier

under pressure
and a tent
of netted wire
I've swept it from

its scaly legs
scattering the rest in air
and borne it
largely silent

to the block.
One flickering
and neutral eye
records the underside of bushes

and something
of the upturned sky.
Some code obscurer still
demands two blows

with handy stick
hard down
across the crown —
local anaesthetic.

My slow, loose-headed
axe with splinters
comes down twice
then once again

slicing the unwilling skin,
a matted thread of feathers.
Splashing blood
across the grass

this lump, this residue
of muscle

at the far end of my arm
begins to flop away

downhill towards the river.
Claws contract
and stiffen in my wrist.
I string her there

with baling twine
an hour or so
in the orange tree.
And later still

the house's airs
simmer with crisp
and cloudless skin
clear gravy and potatoes.

I'm sipping
ice-cold lemonade
and stare
towards the river.

The Elegist

Sleek, dark-suited
as if on the payroll
and with an undertaker's
nervousness of hands

he has touched down this morning
having smelt out the news.
No poet's death
can possibly evade him —

the shifty
sentimental eye,
the steady nose for grief.
Sidelong in the silence

of oregon and stone
he places like an usher
the mourners either side —
remembering old photos,

guessing from the clothes.
Later at the graveside
the breeze cannot
unslick his hair;

his eyes assume
the texture of the sky
and in the rhetoric
of dust and ashes

his images
begin to harden.
A necessary friendship blooms.
Saturday next

their two names meet
across a matter
of four or five stanzas —
though one is always

better known
the printer's ink
unites them nicely
over coffee in the morning sun.

Grand Remonstrance

So much she never
could abide

so much always
to resent

the sulkiness
of mother's teats

the boy next door
astride her scooter

a teacher's random
sudden justice

the tardy flowering
of her breasts

the unfair cycles
of the moon

the owlish eye
of Mr Sims

over her shoulder
as she typed

the gossip that stopped
as she drew near it

the vague delays
of a fiancé

leaning on
the town's opinion

the wedding with relatives
thrice-removed

the uninvited
winsome babies

the hardwon 13-
carat ring

the three-day honeymoon
and then

suddenly
her own two children

the martyrdom
of 3 a.m.

the thoughtless toys
and dirty curtains

smears across
the morning light

the silences
that each child kept

seeking to
outlast her own

the son who sideslipped
out of school

the daughter year
by year   resuming

her mother's skin
the husband too

his daily leavepass
to the world

the false compliance
of his slippers

and then the last
two years in bed

unvisited
and fingering

the soiled card-index
in her head

of grievance going
decades back

to taunts and snubs
in corridors

snideness in
the vivid playground

and so to a slab
of immaculate granite

the lengthening rancour
of the grave

six feet down
and now at last

the stunning
equity of death.

Anthems

Ragged static
from an old loudspeaker
as flags go up and stiffen
under clouds of all kinds
and troops turn always at 90 degrees
to the same lean esperanto

and born from the pen
of the one composer
(see also under *operetta*)
they are scored to be played in dented metal
by village bands
in the key of G

the words likewise
to be sung out of tune
by choirs of yet
unbroken children
each line the work of the one librettist
not unknown to vaudeville.

Floating up from all
the flagpoles of the world
they harmonise in G —
and tie themselves
immutably
to skylines and the weather.

Seven Sins

Superbia

One skimmed smooth
as a bowling green
is married to another

feckless
with its broken car
and thistles in the wind.

Invidia

Glossed and clean
as if from a
foreign magazine

her long Mercedes slides in off the street
and through
compliant doors.

Ira

At half past ten
a muffled fugue
for two ascending voices — then

thicker sounds the walls
will not allow. Always
a child begins to cry.

Acedia

Convulsing
on the freeway in
a cat yields up a life.

The rush hour veers
a fraction right
and keeps on for the sky.

Avaritia

Dreaming at night of other journeys
tanned and languid
with foreign lovers

they wake up still
in bartered rooms. One roof tree
holds it all together.

Gula

Sunday night   a walk at dusk
fast food
from all the gathered doorways —

limbs
of a thousand chickens
sweated in cooking oil.

Luxuria

Two shadows on a blind
undress.
It is the third

across the street
who feels her lips
move on his skin.

from Seven Addresses

Back beneath covers
he feels the days spread either way
between weekends of children;
feels too the space in bed beside him —
taken now and then
by women stiff as folded napkins
or wide with whisky and late confession.
The water in the cistern
climbs back to its level.

Tomorrow night his children
will take a room each side.
Already he hears their invisible breathing —
remembering in advance
the distances at breakfast,
mornings hunched in the wind
on sidelines, the afternoons
of circling horses.

Our lady of the caustic eyes
and modern marriage
has found her way back to it.
The roué of the late-night bars
takes ten years off his age midweek
and at weekends is father of two,
fitted to the street again —
eyes between the split venetians
grudgingly confirm it.

In all the colder reaches of the bed
he cannot now recall
one detail of her body
nor of his wife
                    unless perhaps
those lips drawn tight
behind a fly-wire door
                    each Sunday
taking back the children.

Falling away at last into darkness,
he remembers months before
crying *darling* to his pillow
and thinking of no one.

Weather

Warm not hot
A morning somehow
The colour of ivory

The dew still lifting in the air
A distant taste
Of haze beyond the river.

Three Brahman bulls
Beneath a Moreton Bay
All stare one way

Ignoring the horses.
We stop at the old
Sharefarmer's house.

There is a twist
Of roofing iron
Some tangled wire

And a patch
Of pale cement
(The creamery or meathouse).

Five poles support
The rough-sawn rooms
For thirty years

Transparent —
The name also
Impossibly clear.

Three bulls across the gully
Do not move or
Watch us leave.

Mornings like these
I can almost believe
The weather goes on

Without us.

Clairvoyant in Autumn

The days between my
death and burning
will be three perfect

autumn days —
word spreading quietly
over the wires —

three days just slightly
more intense
as I weigh at the edge

of my friends' concentration.
They do not like
what I imply

inert and waxen
dressed for work
and patient in a box.

They do not like
the dark tie once again
the slow ride to the edge of town

the words sincere or otherwise
the impure silence
the thought of fire

and woodash
mixed in with the bones.
As friends split up in the car park

there will be
on the mountains
the shadows of cloud.

Premeditations

'Family of Four / Shot Dead'

With a pull-through and the .22
on the back step as the moon
breaks over the stockade barn

the afternoon
is trembling in his fingers:

the banker's shallow eyes
the barman's face a net of blood
the gate still scraping in the dirt
the dog stretched tight
in half-wit welcome.

Somewhere behind him
straight through timber
cracked plates are going
back to shelves
well past resentment now.
Four cups shiver on their hooks
and soap-raw palms on faded cotton
defer the small reward
of tea.

And at the table
two slight girls with lunar faces
are one day more
grown used to silences

fatigue and long division
brought back thirty miles by bus
on gravel they turn through
even in dreams.

Out in the house paddock
the shadows of harrows
are merging with the earth
as if it weren't already
mortgaged to the wind.
Fingers ply more smoothly now
the flannel cloth and pull-through —
and the moon has gone completely.

Inside behind him
three iron beds
are passive and accepting

as they will be again
when only the dog
will wake on its chain to morning.

Playboys of 1938

Photos in a
Shoebox curling
Four young men
In shirts and flannels
The open photo-
Graphic faces
Lifeboats and an
Airvent's throat
Between sets on
The Indian Ocean
Engines continuing
Under the shoes
A girl looks in
From out of the frame
Black tie by night
With alto sax
And *Dancing in the*
Dark outside
A jazzy laugh
Thrown over the rail
Last to go
They crowd the piano
And ten years on
The whole of a tune
Will still live for one
In diffident fingers
So too the starch
Of innocent sheets
The texture of a

Cabin's ceiling
The morning skyline
Through a porthole
Three weeks more
At the Folies Bergère
They'll be toasting King Peter
Incognito
Champagne by magnum
Governess French
Vive le roi
Des slaves royaux!
Night by night
The northward engines
Ferry them gracefully
Under the moon
Together with
Those salty moments
Up at the bow
A brunette nestled
Underarm
Plays them fleetly
Each by turn
Resisting what
They do not try
There is one trip
In all their lives
Buried now
In Crete, Tobruk
Or forty years
Forgetting

Grafton

Shortcutting to the Tuesday sales
down streets that kept the season trimmed
and others where the shells of cars
collapsed into paspalum
we'd cruise by in my father's Buick
the towers where sentries walked the sky
and batons worked in silence thirty years
on a few men at a line's far end
or trapped maybe in levels of ourselves
I could not quite yet see in dreams
outside the Tuesday sales,
the moan of gathered cattle
muffled through the glass.

Small Song

In books and in
the Sunday paddocks
lambs leap for him

he has them by their sound
not yet the word.
Later in his highchair

he'll tilt away to sleep
idyllic and still sucking
a short loin bone.

Fledgling

A magpie washed
Into a gutter
A mouse the cat has shaken out —

You look on as I dig them in
Your chatter a little
Harder and higher.

You will not be picked up —
Your small bone-cage
Has wriggled from my grip

To stare.
There is a word
I don't quite mention.

Why should I ache
As well as smile
To see you leaping on the beach

And lifted in your grandpa's arms?
Sending the shovel down
I watch the truths that circle in your face

Agreeing not to meet.

Yellowing Paper

1880–1980

Staring from your
varnished frames
in a thousand folk museums,
town clerks or
small-school headmasters
stiff as your collars
or portly with watch-chains,
it seems I have to take you
seriously at last —
with your wives as tough
as they'd have to be
with their thirteen
annual children;
the seven or so remaining
stare straight from the frame
a little smeared
by insects under glass.
You smell of stale cardboard
and yellowing paper;
your thoughts, I fear,
are faintly pompous.
I read them in these
frail editions
which want 'a tidy GIRL,
to be useful' or
'two smart lads' as
'general servants'.

Your shapely
long parentheses
would bring a continent to order.
Your sexual life
though vigorous surely
does not bear thinking on:
a snort or neigh
with scent of cigar,
your women stiff
as their mothers' maxims —
and somewhere too
a whiff of the brothel.
In the next world now
with all your obsolescence
lovingly arranged around you
(the christening robes
like tiny shrouds,
the chamber-pots and worn-out mangles)
your evening hours
are sewn into a cushion
together with the sound
of Dickens.
My grandmother, 99,
sat once in your parlours
and heard the pianos,
the steady andantes
of gifted slim girls
awaiting the promise
of serial fiction,
the facts
running on beyond that ...

Always
      the smell
of mucilage.
Silverfish already
stitch between our dreams.

Roots and Branches

1.

It climbs
five generations high
to vanish into clouds:
you hang there with your cousins
among the lower boughs.

2.

Sideways too
it holds you fixed
and focussed at its point:
the leftward lean of generations
weighing in on you.

3.

And back along
the distaff side
those sternly-seated ladies,
handing down their
genes as heirlooms,
giving up their names.

4.

Long rows of fertility
run right off the page:
the once-a-year
soft-swelling wombs,
the three-foot boxes
not accepted.

5.
Propriety,
propinquity,
impatience in the blood:
the marriage bracket,
filled and knotted,
straightens to a point.

6.
Striding down
the upper boughs
all men recite their names —
and as the mantis
mates and prays
he's eaten up
and thrown away.

7.
And then that pruning
of the stem:
the aunts who line
a drawing room,
the sons swept off
by chance or bugle,
the misadventures
of the womb.
A clerk presents
a pistol to his head.
The genes step neatly sideways
and veer on down their name.

8.

Certificates of union,
advent and farewell:
we certify ourselves and bear
the long indifference
of clerks.
You find a deck
of thieves and whores,
she finds an earl far back;
parvenu and blueblood both
run out into conjecture.

9.

Vanishing
from left to right
already we are lost,
a kind of high slipstream.
Housewives, blacksmiths,
surgeons, mayors,
maiden aunts and clerks ...
they and all their days
like clouds
are passing through me still.

from NX 250

Taken on your birthday, turning 28, they force you north
    across the range
And into the hulls of planes — which only two weeks back
    you'd seen
Sowing troops across a sunset; then cattletruck you north
    once more,

Three days straight, no food or pause, a bucket for
Shit at the centre. The guards gun down a woman for
    offering you bread.
At Stalag VIIB at last they siphon officers from men;

Behind the wire of Oflag IX four years' waste —and half a
    life — begin.
Retreats by now are orderly; there is a list for escapees
And your turn never quite comes round. You live on
    German consommé
(One cabbage leaf per gallon), black bread, sour cheese to
    bless the Sabbath,
The enemy cut back to size — latrine rats and body lice.
You stalk the BBC each night with crystal and catswhisker

And try your high school Latin out on Mussolini's speeches,
Each guard a stiff barometer to where the great campaigns
    are turning,
Heinz and Herman stooped somewhat by Stalingrad and
    Alamein;

Though near the end in petulance they work you on the
     roads outside
Sewn flat by Yankee planes. *'Befehl ist Befehl'*, as they say,
But you were officers and English, deserving of Geneva —

Other wire had crueller logic. *'Kriegsgefangener'* not 'Killed',
The coupon letters come and go, your sister burgeoning
     down south and you
Increasingly an uncle, the censorship imposed each way

No tighter than your own reserve, always a closer prison —
Though once the Red Cross battled through (with
     Cadbury's in pocket)
And took your photograph: 10th November '42,
Formally (how else?) At Ease, a damp (Bavarian?) ridge in
     the distance,
A row of elms and no wire seen, your boots as always
     shockingly clean,
The corners of your mouth turned down in pure self-discipline.

A stare not so much more intense was found on Japanese at
     Cowra,
Climbing on the wire to die. When British tanks roll through
     the wire
No one is quite released.

Opiates of Autumn

So much golden alchemy
and still no magic stone.

The doctor's smile
fades off into a shrug

levels of fat pressure of blood
tiredness of a kidney.

Week by week
the world grows brittle

and everything around us with it
houses days and children.

Friends as solid as their handshakes
blow smokily away

the space they leave
is all about us.

So many centuries
of April

and these last stained
and spacious days

opiates of autumn.

Busful of Widows
National Library

A wind off the mountains
has swept the marble clean.
In coats of muted gabardine
and scarves against the wind
they move in twos and threes
towards the door,
not saying much.
Reg and Fred and Olley
are spaces in a bed,
an ache that fades like anaesthetic,
a space in the memory.
Freedom it seems
is made up of absence
and a landscape on the move
through glass. Busfuls
at this moment
are fanning out from Sydney
nosing up mountains
or skirting the coasts.
A fringe of grey
escapes the wimpled scarf.
Best years of my life, says one,
have been since Dougie died.
A quick look up
at Grecian columns
then in

through automatic doors.
Obscure and perched in polaroid
the driver scans his paper
and still an engine rumbles on
conditioning the air.

The City of Curves

The city of curves is also a marriage
with all destinations equally far,
the gearshift neutral there between you.
It is, let's say, a rainy evening
a twilight bent with heavy boughs
the garbage hopeful at the kerb
the wine behind you not too cheap
and not too good to give.
Ranges fill the rearview mirror
the city map's blown up to life
signposted by the dead.
Children jettisoned back there
are sleeping neatly now
the sitter browsing on your shelves.
The host by nine has given up
and carries in the soup.
By torchlight as the anger thickens
how is it that you smile?
In the city of curves and destinations
you dream together all night through
of making the right mistake.

Broken Ballad

The faithful sailing
In their graves
Sing praises to the Lord

As doubters restless
Row by row
Grow leaner and more bored.

Believers patient
Underground
Await the lifting kiss

And sceptics stare
Into the stone —
They had expected this.

Equally
The planet swings them
Round a failing sun

Till doubt and faith
Are frozen iron
And metaphors are gone.

Recess

Hands warm round
a cracking mug
and far off in a corner

I am watching
forty-seven deaths
in a staffroom at recess

and forty-seven lives also
combustive in a room.
Conversation

comes in gusts
and forty-seven lives are snuffed
with one grenade

or swept off at a gasp
together with the city.
More slowly and more likely

it comes in wards and homes
where nurses watch a screen go blank
or daughters at a bedside

survive the breath not taken.
It comes in going down
politely and forever

sideways on a public street,
a broken parcel in the chest —
or airborne out on country roads

and floating for a tree.
Eleven ten.
The air is tight

with cigarettes and laughter;
the deputy
is signalling for quiet,

 a clattered spoon
upon a cup.
This coffee's nearly

halfway gone —
black, no sugar,
warm and thin.

The Motto

Seventeen and
six foot two
and it's merely an issue
of uniform how —
army, navy
or police ...
textbook shoulders
fleckless face
hair swept neatly
into place
and handsome enough
to stare from a poster
resolute into the future

which twelve years on
has been and gone
drinking at this
class reunion.
There is that
thickening throughout
the face outspread
and bent at the edges.
Schooner to hand
and gut on the buckle
the marks outside
and those within
go back to a domestic
a phone call followed

up with boots
delivered to the
groin and chin.
Rape to murder …
Cat up a tree.
You sense the dent
below the skin.
Finish all hours
And get on the piss
A few of y' mates there
Round by the point
With two dozen tins
And a coupla chicks.
He gives his quiet
sidewindow laugh
The wives don't tend
To like it much
and parodies a
midnight call
I got this problem see.
The eyes though smeared
are a cornered stray's
the swearing a tic
to go with the rest.
Gonna get up the Goldcoast
And sit in the sun.
The foam fixed now
and dry on the glass.
Compo should just
Settle the house.
He looks for the bar

then man to man
slaps you with his
twelve years' wisdom:
Stand tall when you have to
Fuck around when you can.

A Line to the City

'Wouldn't mind a
bit of that,'
my father had a
way of saying
out between towns
in the '38 Buick,
stopping right there
to check a grass
or try the topsoil
on his palm;
one glance would reckon
head per acre,
his own by good sense
focussed now —
breeders on
the hills upriver,
fats downstream
by the abattoir.

*

I'd rather myself
if the season's good
be driving at dusk
a line to the city
and feel the loam
(that deep sea swell)
go down for yards
below the tar,

the sheep illumined
on the hills,
the softer foreign
trees in rows,
the spaced and fading
dams and homesteads,
swift green paddocks
tipped with light.
Half an hour,
a destination,
the freedom to drive,
a ration of petrol ...
all you need
to be bequeathed
a freehold straight
from others' hands,
a shifting silhouette
of gums
still scribbled on the ridges.

Retirement by the Sea

It's not just the cold
in the bones that brings us,
not just the handshake

changed to brick,
a life's allowance of the sea.
The purity of golf or bowls

would be the same elsewhere,
the swell of roofs when leading trumps
beguiling as the waves.

Life, admittedly, down here
leaps up between the fingers —
a lawn with more than three days' growth

is a salesman's five o'clock shadow.
The weathering of gums is endless.
Everywhere flowerbeds

etched in cement
are keeping the worlds apart.
Men for years commute at nine

to levels of tomato,
those gardens with their
older truths

and fruit for half a street.
How else might one
be called from work?

The long fidelities at lunch
and garnered irritations
are poised as on a lifted fork,

a balance to be shaken only
by children and the children's children,
a two-day southerly buster.

They say, half-joking at the clubs, we're thinning out in style
(invisibly replenished);
the men go first, the widows for a moment stunned

take to the telephone.
The signs if one walks out at six
are surgeries and land for sale.

The cemetery at last
is clipped and fenced,
the headstones from a distance

scattered like gulls
on the long ridge facing the sea
which in itself holds no great interest.

Sometimes, briefly,
waking at night,
we wonder why we've come.

from The River

(1977–   )

Looking up
without a moon
you're nearly all
potential still
and see no reason
why you shouldn't
skim across the
milky way
somewhere out
along your life
the speed of light
a stingy limit
set there to be
broken down.

At seven already
you have a past —
close-ups, flashes,
filed at random,
unseen, half-lost
between your parents,
their weekday grey
of bills and washing
the future ache
of your nostalgia.
A child alone
between them both,
your words by far

outrun your years:
you deal them with
a subtle touch:
'I've got a power
over you, you know …
Only I
can make you a grandpa.'

And once a year
beside the river
you stand back from
your cousins' skills,
the horse a stodgy
means of transport,
definitely
short on wings.
Rowed on your river's
clouds and mountains
you drift a finger
in the stream,
prattle of death
on other planets
and do not quite
tie up untouched.

South again
in the city of curves
a missile soaring
on a screen,
a grainy clip
from Hiroshima,
can leave you staring

mute for minutes,
searching out
not yet with words
an upstream promise
from your forebears:

a leisurely
and single death
surrounded by your heirs.

Tinnitus

*There is no specific treatment for tinnitus aurium, The patient
however should not be abandoned.*

Medical text

Some hear a hissing
a buzzing or ringing
a sigh of the sea
inside its shell

molecular motion
of the air
static from a
closed-down speaker.

Some hear a higher
horizon of crickets
an octave up
from moonlit reeds

the top C of
a trumpet solo
overtones lifting
on fathomless air.

For some it's more
a faulty tap
a rumour somewhere
in the plumbing

a fluorescent
light left on

deep in the heart
of a public building.

A few hear God's
insistent whisper
opaque always
as the world

the upper registers
of pain
just that half tone
short of madness.

To wake at three
and read the ceiling
is more than a smear
of the infinite;

out there, that higher
stave of crickets
and death I know
is one flicked switch

and after that, white noise.

My Mother's God

My mother's God
has written the best
of the protestant proverbs:

you make the bed
you lie in it;
God helps him

who helps himself.
He tends to shy away from churches,
is more to be found in

phone calls to daughters
or rain clouds over rusty grass.
The Catholics

have got him wrong entirely:
too much waving the arms about,
the incense and caftan, that rainbow light.

He's leaner than that,
lean as a pair of
grocer's scales,

hard as a hammer at cattle sales
the third and final
time of asking.

His face is most clear
in a scrubbed wooden table
or deep in the shine of a

laminex bench.
He's also observed at weddings and funerals
by strict invitation, not knowing quite

which side to sit on.
His second book, my mother says,
is often now too well received;

the first is where the centre is,
tooth for claw and eye for tooth.
Whoever tried the other cheek?

Well, Christ maybe,
but that's another story.
God, like her, by dint of coursework

has a further degree in predestination.
Immortal, omniscient, no doubt of that,
he nevertheless keeps regular hours

and wipes his feet clean on the mat,
is not to be seen at three in the morning.
His portrait done in a vigorous charcoal

is fixed on the inner
curve of her forehead.
Omnipotent there

in broad black strokes
he does not move.
It is not easy, she'd confess,

to be my mother's God.

Gravity's End

Another galaxy
collapses.

Gently now
the shock arrives,

the swallowing of stars
a ripple passing through us.

Density and mass
collide

as, stretched to a thread,
by gravity's end,

you slip across
that last of all horizons.

As aeons concentrate
to nothing

your atoms find
their final closeness

buried in the stars.

Footwork

'Slow slow
Quick quick slow ...'
Two years short
Of rock-and-roll
The boys of Remove
Are learning to dance
Resisting by turn
The need to be girl
As Mrs McBride
With tartan and pearls
Turns at the centre
Declaring the step
To boys thirteen
Who've not shaved yet.
An early frost
Comes down on the gym
As climbing ropes
And boxing ring
Are swung aside
For patent leather
Or what the future's
Thought to wear;
The dinner suits
And girls with style
The anchored palm
The aspidistra
An open deck
With lacquered sky
The ballroom now

A carousel
A roundabout of
Doubting couples
Hands and knees
Still scuffed from tackles.
Eric and Gerald
Thirteen still
With Cyril and Jim
are scraping their soles.
Discovered by
The final bar
They leap apart
So no one knows
Who led who followed
Or who in the foxtrot
Known as life
Will stand and wait
With crumpled hankie,
Sweated palms.
'Goodnight boys,'
The matron says.

Tomorrow the gloves
Are on again.

An Offertory

Walking the block on a Sunday evening
a low sky curved and held with streetlights
the plane trees filled, bent down with rain
you stroll in the wealth that is patient around you
the garbage somehow stiffened in air
vertical, weightless, in galvanised light
the yoghurt cartons crushed or broken
the limbs of chickens stripped and split
the finished news pierced through with fishbones
wet with coleslaw, glazed with fat.
You too are a part of all that you walk through
you find the same three-colour brochures
the envelopes for power and phone
and yet between the floating layers
there is a single shredded cry
that no one else can quite receive.
The air tonight is rich with refuse
filled with the texture and thickness of cream
and over the rise there'll be evensong somewhere
this garbage also a kind of praise.

Findings

The sewage climbs through open rock
The sky comes down across the block

The politician's sideways smile
Is one day more deferred from trial

The office towers of Crime & Class
Are made of honesty and glass

The strongroom at police HQ
Is down always an ounce or two

The dealer in his shallow bed
Is still ambitious five months dead

The lawyer takes his lunch at two
Straight cocaine with harbour view

The addict strolls through deadlocked doors
Hauls out a cord but not the cause

Girls in doorways cold and calm
Sell their legs to feed their arm

Two parents watch the skyline frown
The sewage rises the sky comes down

American Sketches

1. L.A. Freeways
Banking and swooping over the houses
And heat-pressed boulevards with palms
Swinging wide of the towers downtown
Those mirrors filled with the dry sierras
You sense just once a stoppage in the film
The ziggurats of Hollywood
City of instant ruins

2. Anthony Braxton at Kimballs, San Francisco
Mathematics of the vacuum
A newer music of the spheres
Spun by the angels
Of shattered glass
Bent by fibres of the street
An ebony of wind and wire
Blowing back in from the future

3. San Francisco Poets Congress, November 14
Light Poets / Black Poets / Poets of the Milky Way
Sun Poets / Moon Poets / Poets of the People
Zen Poets / Space Poets / Elders of Tomorrow
Bay Poets / Gay Poets / Spontaneous Concrete
Talking Pictures / Endless Rainbows / Gangs of the Kosmos
Street Poets / Beat Poets / Language Bop Scat Wow
Be In It / Call 824-3266 / Now

4. Philadelphia—New York on the New Jersey Turnpike

'Longest Italian graveyard in the world'
The hitmen restless in cement
As fat white jets float down beside you
In the white world of the cracking towers
Where even the smoke from factory stacks
Is billowing white as sheets on a line
And the skies of East Manhattan are rising on the wind

5. Corner Broadway and 48th Street

'Ya gotta dime lady? Ya gotta dime?'
An old man rattles his plastic cup
The Broadway matron swirled in fur
Deflects the tackle New York style
And yanks her matched designer poodle
Yapping backwards after her
'C'mon now, come outa that, ya goddam little cutie pie'

6. M.J.Q. at the Blue Note, New York City

A century of modern jazz
Shimmering on stage between them
Two continents in balance there
The quarter tones of Senegal
Crying in the hammered scales
The stones and choirs of Chartres cathedral
Singing in the chords

7. Anecdote of New York City, told in Toronto later

And suddenly the street is empty
'Give us y' fuckin' money, man'
And a gun just under the armpit
Your mind as empty as the street

'Only got Canadian, sorry'
'Don't worry. You have a nice vacation, man'
And beats it up the street

8. Downtown San Francisco from Oakland Bridge at 10 p.m.
And now you see
These ice-cube lights, these pearl mosaics
In all their fluorescent levels
Stacked up loosely floor by floor
Are a sudden and luminous
Japanese paper
Nagasaki the night before

Four in the Morning, Year of the Peace

Somehow always you're out on patrol,
a 'search and destroy', your son and you only.
He's got the FN. You've got nothing.

The jungle is abstract, indefinite height,
not quite seen but specific with insects
and neither particularly day or night.

Next by a kind of filmic splice
there's a VC standing in your path, bent, like your son,
by a sub-machine gun, an AK 47 maybe,

which he holds at your line of head and chest.
He's a VC clearly but just thirteen
and somewhere from the west of Sydney.

You stare one way. He stares back.
Your son, you realise, is waving a weapon
as if by inherited inadvertence

at the other boy's stomach.
Under the VC's neutral skin something already is
foreign to doctrine. He starts to turn

as if to go a long way back and start again.
'Go on!' you yell. 'Go get the bastard!'
Shaking his nine-year skinny shoulder. A short burst then

but still remote, close in volume, distant in origin.
It whips up uselessly into the leaves
like gravel tossed in a lobby of glass.

The other boy turns and fires without thought,
ripping your son across the chest, jolting him backwards
into your arms. You're sitting up now.

He stands right there. 'Bad dream, Dad?' then climbs in wounded
close beside you; shivers a little, say
two or three times; and almost at once

is stiff on the pillow.

Clarence Lyric
for Alec and Penelope Hope

Surrounded by his
Pills and bottles
The old man's heaped
In bed at last
Washed in sidelong
From the world
Which circles seaward
With his past

Carpet snakes
With rats and swallows
Weave their close
Dependent lives
Silverfish
Invade the paintings
Whiteants hollow
Out the piles

A grandson and his
Wife move in
Rational with
Paint and saw
Three children spread
Into the rooms
Banging through the
Cedar doors

One soon lost
To outer paddocks
Another buoyant
On her smile
A third obscurely
Stalled by fiction
In a chair not
Quite in style

Snakes slide from
The long verandah
Rats go back
To tractor sheds
All morning through
The polished glass
A man stares outwards
From the dead

Sees the river
Skimmed with wind
Hears the children
Start to fight
The afternoon
Goes on forever
The westward pools
Are filled with light

Toona Australis

1.

Two men at the end of the cedar trade
two men with flattened leather faces
stand for a lens in front of a hut.
Shovel-bearded, one with a pipe,
wide felt brims turned up to the light,
their minds are filled a day at a time
with crowns of cedar against the sky
and the super feet sawn from trunks at a glance.
Their bellies are rich with salt beef and damper
their nose with tobacco and three months' sweat.
They have just finished lunch the photographer tells us
—and maybe a species —
and yet are in no way different from us.

2.

The homestead high
on its river bluff

a dining room
all done with cedar

five sides of six
in deep red panels

complete with candles,
silverware ...

'All cut on the place,'
they tell you twice

as the beef arrives.
'There's still one left

old Henry reckons
out there back of

Middle Top.
Have to take you

next time round.'
A single tree

in a creek's head somewhere
a final crown

in the passing sky.
And back you go

for thirty years
to help them with the lie.

3.
Ten years on
from Phillip's flag,
the bugle and gunshot
of Sydney Cove,
they are spreading already,
the coastal cutters,
breasting the bars

of the tricky rivers,
riding the stillness
on lower reaches.
Two-man saws
and whetted axes
step ashore
and are lost in the forest,
seeking the great trees
stripped for winter
or (seen from bluffs
in the heavy air)
flagrant with their new
pink spring growth.
As Sheffield steel
swings low to ground
a nib is inked
in Government House —
'Such logs or planks
that are not licensed
are hereby seized
for Government use —
sassafras and
cabbage palm
go with them to
the earth, each log
then snigged and worried
to a pit
where two young poachers
going straight
snap a chalkline
tight between them
then flense their log

to market planks,
the one above
to keep the line,
the one below
to haul down hard
a sawdust rich with the
'smell of roses'
reddening his
Irish hair.
A feint to the south
then north by rivers
(Hastings, Manning,
Clarence, Tweed)
running the shoals
and into the silence.
In fifty years
they find an end;
the trees no longer
shed their seasons
(so many circuits
of the sun),
the last logs drawn
by bullock sweat
or rolled into a
springtime fresh
to wash against
a downstream chain,
or dry maybe
on flats for farmers,
slip a line
for the open sea.
The cedar, squared,

is shipped as ballast
north to Bombay,
Home to London.
Sawn for panelling
or tables
it rises through
a craftsman's plane
and through a pane
of pure French polish
the red's as deep
as wine or blood,
so soft your thumbnail
leaves its name.
In Richmond scrub
some scraps lie still.
'It burns,' they wrote,
'with a lambent flame.'

Monologues for '88

1. Dispatch
Ramornie 1841

Having received from several sides
divers accounts of savage crimes
committed on the Clarence River
by native Aboriginees
and the scattering of cattle
with numerous other depredations
most notably the robbery of
a shepherd's hut on Ramornie station
a party of settlers suitably armed
was raised up by my constable
and under my express command
entrapped an evening camp of blacks
on the banks of the Orara
complete with sundry gins and young.
Our discipline began at dawn.
Two men of ours alas
were somewhat pierced by spears.
The 'lords of the soil' as they are called
took to the river by the score
and were shot as they swam;
many were I understand
to be seen downstream a few days later
against the wharves of the Settlement.
More late intelligence confirms
the felonies were practised by

a rogue named Lynch without a doubt.
The blacks it appears have yet to commit
a single crime or depredation
upon Ramornie or thereabouts.

2. The Philosophical Remark
Grafton 1980
'In the long run, y' know,
we all get rolled every once in a while,

say every thousand years or so,'
tamping the cigarette.

'We're all a packa bastards really,
Julius Caesar, Billy the Norman,

no way outta that, I guess,'
looking to northwards,

striking the match.

3. The Long Agistment
Yulgilbar 1842
i.
We said that we had made war upon them because they
had killed white people but that now our anger was gone
and that we wished to live in peace.

We said that we wanted nothing in their country but the
grass and would leave them their kangaroos, their
opossums and their fish.

We told them that if they would not rob or injure our
people nor kill our sheep that no person would harm them
but, on the contrary, would give them bread when they
came to the stations.

The sun was now sinking: therefore,
after distributing our pocket knives, our handkerchiefs and
such articles of our dress as we could spare we told them we
must go. They all rose and accompanied us.

Toolbillibam walked before and with much care parted the
long grass with his hand and cleared away all obstacles from
our path.

ii.
And hardly knowing
yet ourselves

we did not speak
of cooks and masons

nor how by then
Toolbillibam

would be to stationhands
King Billy

nor further on
of all the miles

of wire we'd need
to square the acres

nor the roll or two
that would more than serve

a second century
to close

the Yulgilbar
Reserve hard by

John Hardie's mine
for white asbestos

nor quite of how
King Billy's men

would see that sweeping
of the hand

and coin the myth
of how we'd asked

for nothing but the grass.

4. Ballad for Joseph Hartmann
        Copmanhurst 1951
Joseph Hartmann was his name,
'Old Black Joe' for short,
coined by schoolbus choirs of kids
because his dad had caught

a touch of tar at Yulgilbar
and a long asbestos cough;
he worked a farm downriver now.
My parents warned me off.

Their rumour ran him sideways to
the blacks who rode the bus
with portwine wrapped in newspaper;
they swigged it watched by us

and richly slurred their syllables
way past our final stop.
Joe asked me to his birthday once.
A stockman dropped me off.

The house was roughsawn walls and floor
on eighty acres rented
polished to a moral shine
my mother would have envied.

He was my best friend for a while
and sent a letter once,
my second year at boarding school
when he'd left school six months.

The hand, well-spelt, had worked the roads
some time before his beard.
I'm sure I must have written back
before he disappeared.

5. *Armidale Tableau*
1968

Driving north
through the City of Schools
(and two cathedrals)
where fifteen years have slid away
since you in your grammar school
socks and shoes
and your boarder's allowance of Sunday
scavenged on the city tip
keeping your Speedwell close to hand
your eyes throughout acutely left
from the place where the dump turned human
the twisted hair, the Kiwi shine
of faces black as your shoes for chapel
the hammered-out four-gallon tins
the place where sheets of roofing iron
were vertical with doorways
and toothless women in them
their jumpers with the elbows gone
(what was it then, what piece of scrap,
you pedalled off with down the gravel?)
as now you pause at the town's main square
(Land Rovers, utes, a couple of Daimlers)
and see over there the granite cross
to the Great War Christian dead
and two black youths on the steps below it
sharing a bottle wrapped in the news
(Penfolds Sherry, Seppelts Port)

till finally the traffic clears
and you slip across with your window wound
past granite steps and the hardened names
the Crofts and Dangars, Whites and Wrights
as the younger one there
with lavender shirt and brylcreemed hair
falls away sideways under the cross
and something like motor oil pours from his palm
the older one yanking him savagely back
and soundlessly you hear the stain
'Sit up, you fuckin' boong'
and in no time at all you are free in the country
foot to the floor past the protestant homesteads
quiet below skylines with their windbreaks of pine.

The Problem

The problem is,
he reads too much,
stays up later
than he should,
turning back to
George the Third
and hearing in the
moon and rapids
whispers of a
scattered tribe,
the truths that lie
between the pages,
silent truths
that ruin sleep.
The homestead poles
grow insecure,
as if some hawser
had been loosened.
The fence posts shift
within their holes
and cattle rise
to graze in air;
the hardwood floor
grows light beneath him.
And having nowhere
else to go
each night the house
will lift its timbers,
the soil below

grow scarred and blurred,
although indelible
with sweat.
Each night for hours
upon its moorings
the homestead hangs
suspended there,
a kite of weatherboard
in air ...

And only dawn
with all its weight
can bring it down again.

Acid Paper
for Jan Lyall

The voices of the dead are growing frailer.
Along the high kilometres of shelves
they are quarrelling in silence
and eaten from the edges.
The stiffening that held the tree
resistant to its years of wind
has made the pages crack.
The past that rides such brittle shallows
is rubbed to rust between the fingers
and thoughts contract towards the centre
shrinking from the light and air.
The works of Tennyson and Browning,
the newsprint that began a war,
the tracts that promised
English heavens, pornographies Morocco bound,
the German of *Das Kapital*
are threatened by a pure amnesia
impartial as the laws of physics.
'More durable than bronze,' said Horace,
and set it quickly down.
Dulce et decorum est ...
mens sana in corpore sano ...
A poet may outlive his time,
more recently his work also —
and feel it crumble in the palm
before his bones are in the furnace.
Lenses like a dragonfly
are dreaming slowly at the surface.

We choose the past to take on with us
just as we have always done
and leave the rest behind like weather ...
that summer of the year 'fourteen' —
and certain nouns abandoned with it ...
this sheet beneath the printer's kiss
vivid with its swift illusions.

The Opening of Parliament House, 1927

The speeches done, the crowd has thinned
away into its waiting Fords.
Two matrons and an eight-year-old
are strolling slowly through the frame ...
seven flagpoles each with flag
and not the slightest breeze to lift them.
And here in what appears to be
the stubble of a shaven paddock
he is resting quietly with two dogs,
his back against a rolled-up blanket.
The light once more has struck from behind —
an outline of the hat and whiskers,
the face obscured, a dark face darker still.
In his hand a coloured rag,
the Union Jack complete with stars.
The parliament has come from Melbourne
and stands there squarely in a field.
The caption underneath supplies
the honorific line 'King Billy'
... said to be a traditional owner'.
The photograph up top displays
Dame Nellie on a little dais
working on 'God Save the King'-
and Stanley Melbourne Bruce, PM,
waistcoat, watch-chain, at the head of the stairs,
standing vaguely at attention.
The Prince of Wales or Duke of Kent
in battledress salutes his father.
The microphone is tall and awkward

as if no one knew how to use it.
Between this photo and the next,
'King Billy' at the crowd's far edge
has heard the diva's final quaver
splitting in the autumn air.
He calls his dogs and turns to leave
as someone in a suit and hat
shoves something at him on a stick:

'Hey there, Billy, where's y' flag?'

Sixpence
(WA 1933)

Dear little Sixpence
from something like rape
south in the kitchen
and paler of face

stoking the stove
in midsummer heat
told to be grateful
for roof and her keep

you're one of the family
the white woman says
eat in the kitchen
wash down the stairs

you're one of the family
five bob a year
camp on the sleepout
no black kids in here

you say she's the master's
it's happened before
we've five of our own
we don't want any more

we'll pay for a Home
it's better all round
she'll learn to press linen
and beef by the pound

and don't you be fretting
her features are light
if she learns her trade properly
she can marry a white ...

and the sound that returns
as she's driven away
is the echo that Sixpence
still hears from that day

twenty years to the north
her own mother's crying
that missionary chatter
of reading and writing

and a half-brother staring
from down at the creek
who thought she'd be back
by the end of next week

her mother whose voice
was a single crushed note
no permit to travel
no pay for a boat

dead in ten years
and not seen again
for all the good reasons
of government men ...

as in from the coast
an old truck came ...
and slavery had long since
lost track of its name.

Fish with Coffee

Kicking
through the finished leaves
that land beside
an April sky
you stop and watch
this ten-year-old
who half an hour
before maybe
has hooked his
European carp
yanked it from
the lake's khaki
and left it drying
on the grass.
The sun forgives him
on the shoulders
and Christ said Peter
be a fisher of men
and carp we know
eat native fish
and turn our liquid
skies to amber.
'You gonna eat him?'
'Dunno. Maybe'.
And have in mind
a cup of coffee.
The fish is almost
garbage now,
a cancelled colour,

mouth an 0,
a camera's hole
that sucks and shuts
pulsating in the
upturned light.
No hook deforms
those perfect vowels
or interrupts
its mute soprano.
You feel your eye
refuse its stare.
And later take
your cappuccino
gasping
in the autumn air.

The Sound

Four boys stroll in a stormwater channel,
skylarking mildly and shoving at shoulders,
spinning away as if skating the wall,
their sneakers fluent on the stonework
then skidding back towards the water,
a greenish murmur in the middle.
Now, suddenly, a nose has wrinkled
as memory tightens in the nostrils,
a dead sheep on a gravel verge —
but this, despite the white cement,
the hardened light and soft wind rich
with kerosene, is not a road.
The smart remarks continue on,
a light graffiti in the air.
The one called Brett checks out the pipe,
a sideways entry in the stone,
and there, inside, beyond the sun,
is something small ... shapeless as
a sleeping cat ... wrapped, he can see,
in vertical lines, a towel perhaps.
The other three have noticed nothing,
have gone on almost out of hearing.
The light that shatters on the concrete
makes it hard to deal with shade.
Except for the smell, that raw, sweet smell
it could well be a change of clothes
(gym shoes, shorts, a T-shirt, sweater).
Then, not looking up, he calls:
'Hey, you guys ...' before his eyes

have quite adjusted and while the towel
is still a blur — stripes, no colour,
just this hard, discordant smell.
The other three have stooped beside him.
Tomorrow's press will find the words
but not attempt this face that greets them
sightless from its stiffened wrappings
nor catch the cry that is released
from sudden levels of themselves,
a cry without sound and quite without end

as they walk back to Wayne's to ring the police.

New England, 1952

1.

'Do youse stack
or are youse gentry?'
the housemaid says
fresh out from town —
and takes away the soup plates
one by one.

2.

And this always to the boss's son:
'How are yer goin', squire?'
The question high in the early saddle,
the hat obscuring
half the sky.

3.

The houndstooth coat
the jodphurs' skin
the windsor-knotted Sydney tie
as all the careless of the world
go open-necked with gut on buckle.
The Daimler there
outside the pub
shows just the slightest
trace of mud.

4.

There is a choice,
saloon or public,

blood-red carpet
or the tiles.
The Ladies Lounge
is further off again.
The dispossessed
in darker shades
continue in the park.

5.
When Anzac Day's
khaki and brass
swing straight on through
the April air
the men out front
from three pips up
share out the same
half-dozen names.

6.
Homestead widows
back in town
locate the Herald's
lean Vice Regal —
then smile into
an Earl Grey tea
to see a name
they've almost known.

7.
The landscape's mainly
mist and granite,
merinos in the clearing fog;

the homesteads hang
below the ridges,
each one with its line of pines ...
and on the thirty miles between
an MG with its sudden heir,
those slow utilities with dog.

8.
The English, we knew distantly,
could go on doing this forever.

Codicil

And then
when you've acquired the ashes,
that crushed white gravel
in a box,
carry them north to the
Clarence River,
a two-day trip
to close the curve.
Late spring or early summer,
October might be best,
and check before you leave
it's not in flood.
The time, I think, might be
say five o'clock,
just when the shade
comes off the mountain.
The water will
be almost still,
a deep, unending green
with one faint, indecisive breeze
to bend the surface slightly.
The heat by then
will start to lift,
the river start
to fill with evening.
Pause here now together briefly;
then one of you — my son, I think —
will take the box, remove the lid
and in a single, easy sweep

disperse my body on the river.
If done with grace
it ought to make
a long descending curve ...
as if a net were being cast.
You'll hear then
just the slightest sound,
a run of sand across the water,
the near end hitting first
and then
the high reach of the arc.
And when you've finished
this, my son,
I'd have you pause
two minutes more
before you climb the bank again

and let the upstream view
delight your eyes.

My Father in his Silver Frame

1.

And following the main event
there's something not
unlike a party,
friends and family
drinking tea
distributed throughout the house.
A day to celebrate your birth
would generate the same attendance.
I see how you
might stroll among them
group to group
and have no need for introduction.
You might have rung them
all yourself then
suddenly been very late.
All afternoon I seem to hear
the broken edges
of your voice
still talking in a further room.

2.

The children grieve
no doubt of that
but in the rumpus room downstairs
their energy is unreduced.
At the service they
were shaken out — when disbelief
came flooding in;

receding then without a trace
though taking Grandpa with it.
It is a space
they have to deal with
a silent corner
of the room
beyond their quarrel over rules
even as the game continues.

3.
Upstairs the talk
is retrospective,
the need to trace
and trace again
as if with some
collective pencil
the line of doctors and disease
to see just how
despite your age
you didn't simply fall away
between our small mistakes.

4.
But what stays most
is diminution
that disappearance
into air
that sense of how
outside the church
we offered so much less
resistance to the light.
The limbs that filled

a set of clothes,
the firm dry hand
that gripped my own,
are pressed into a
pure abstraction ...
thinner than that
photograph
on the sideboard there for hours,
that tight beginning
of a smile
inside its silver frame.

The Clarence at Copmanhurst

For forty years I've driven past this moment
a half mile down a side road from the tar
this point where two halves of a river meet
where once I know my small limbs must have swum.
Downstream all is tidal, upstream are
the pools, the rapids' lazy conversation.
The lower half moves eastward to the sea,
a single body lifting to the moon
and splits itself around the delta islands,
skylines of cane still tied to half-forgotten
ferries, before it roughens on the bar.
The other ripples downwards from the right
a patterning of sunlight over stones,
down from all the higher pools, the rapids'
measure in between, pools of perch,
freshwater mullet, the cruising little heads
of turtles, the cattle cut off at the knees
and drinking their reflections, the mountains standing
in one side and backing off the other.
To the left there it's a different stillness, another
kind of mullet feeding in the shallows.
The flats downstream run outwards to the hills,
blue lines on a far horizon. It is
a classic day in winter; the midday sun
slows down an hour to warm my southern bones.
The sandstone scarp across the water there
is fledged with trees; they perch in cracks and lean
out dryly from the cliff as if to wave.
On this side it's alluvial, a kind

of shelf from which to view the other bank;
so clearly it's a campsite, this juncture of
the fresh and salt, millennia of smoke.
And somewhere too I hear a story no-one's
heard for years — or no-one that I know.
Dirrangun in her maddened damming might well
have paused here once, retreating on her way
by stages before she vanished into stone.
But it's just this one warm winter's day, one
of a million either side that reach out to the
left and right. There's no one on the main road
now. It must be a tractor downstream somewhere
working on a lucerne flat, that single
jet trail overhead, the whine too far
behind to catch. The sounds from here are low
and equal; like mist they're lifted by the sun
which lets them float and disappear. Who
could know that forty years would make so much
forgetting? I stand here where two rivers meet
and feel them both as separate lives: the upstream
clarity of pools, the downstream salt
of lower reaches heading for the sea.

Kokoda Corrective

It was here young Australian men fought for the first time
against the prospect of the invasion of their country ...

Paul Keating, Kokoda, Anzac Day 1992

... Or first that could be counted any rate
all lined up here underground
and numbered from the right.

The others were a good bit sooner
hundred years or so
their skulls much further out of sight

or overseas in glass.
Old Pemulwuy of the Eora,
now he gave trouble for a time,

dozen years to be exact
and Yagan on the Upper Swan —
his head was souvenired as well, if I recall.

And Windradyne out Bathurst way
required a whiff of martial law
before he saw the light

and Pigeon in the Kimberley,
now there's a bloke who liked a fight.
Good that you could make it, Paul.

Nice to see that someone came.
Not actually the first, not quite,
but damn fine all the same.

Villages Without Umbrellas

The villages are tearing up
their history from the pavement;
the cobblestones

are heavy in their hands,
the gullies of the firing squads
unfailingly remembered.

Goats and pigs are lying dead
beside old women gone to feed them.
School is out. It's time for uncle's shotgun now

and flags are spilling from high windows,
a scud of cloud above them.
Memories have armed themselves

and slouch off for the
ancient corners ...
and down here we don't like it much,

don't like to see it
done in colour,
these people with their

quilted hills
and culture rich as cake at Christmas.
Why aren't they drinking,

we would ask,
good coffee in the morning air
and perched in subtle conversation

beneath umbrellas on the square?

The Lesson
i . m . R.F.B.

What were you doing, Bob,
with everything so elemental
as we bore you on our shoulders

the Brindabellas gone in smoke
a black storm cracking from the east
that cold front slanting in against us

the first rain on our faces
as we looked at the layers of ancient gravels
above which now the coffin's poised

and listened to your voice in poems
the voice we knew
translated by a son and daughter

that great one too by Wallace Stevens
'We live in an old chaos of the sun,
Or old dependency of day and night ...'

the last line struck for you exactly
'Downward to darkness, on extended wings'
and the stretch of pure Ecclesiastes

in the version of 1611 ... 'There is a time ...'
and the jazz band starting up again
the great flower of the tuba

marching away between the graves
with your best three hundred friends.
Smoke haze, rain, the wind, the gravels

and eight long clear-eyed years of dying
Earth, Air
Fire, Water ...

You were teaching us to the end.

Marks on Paper

Between the keyboard and the stave
A hesitation of the pen
Between a chisel and the blow
The first intent is lost again

Between the flautist and the score
There is a pane of mute resistance
Between the palette and the brush
A landscape in its own persistence

An actor steps behind the curtain
Leaves a shadow on the stage
Even his smile in celluloid
Cannot survive a later age

Dancers leave a vanished curve
Poets measure off despair
As voices in the wind keep singing
Marks on paper marks on air

Immoveable Feasts

Twenty-first and twenty-second,
twenty-third and twenty-fourth,
December's birthdays ran in rows
but always fell a fraction short.

The Reverend W. Bracingham
back before the first world war
with his good wife between the sheets
knew what the end of March was for.

Other seasons passed them by
circling through the Christian year.
The Reverend W. Bracingham
was always notably severe

if tenderly his wife in bed
(most often in the early spring)
might gently push herself against him.
She'd feel the sharp and sudden sting

of his rebuke. 'My dear,' he'd say,
'All in good time; you need not fear.
We tried it at the end of March.
It's not that special time of year.'

Yes, late March and autumn fires,
she had them often in her head:
the Reverend W. Bracingham
so warmly vigorous in bed.

Rebecca on the twenty-first,
Samuel on the twenty-second,
Rachel on the twenty-third
and James, more accurately reckoned,

appearing on the twenty-fourth -
just a fraction short of six.
Reactions downstairs in the hall,
though pious still, were brief and mixed.

'Four will be enough,' he said
and looked up sternly at the sky —
and never quite could understand
his wife as March went drifting by.

Rebecca, Rachel, Sam and Jim,
each child, she thought, is like a gift —
but God, for reasons of His own,
has kept from us the twenty-fifth.

'Self-discipline,' the Reverend said,
'is like the stiffness in the starch.'
'Yes, dear,' said his lovely wife,
remembering the end of March.

Ulcer

The acids of dissatisfaction
turn themselves about;
they focus and begin to scour.

A fibre-optic in the throat
is checking for the wounds.
The sourness here

is excess to requirements,
a metal taste of 3 a.m.
as sleep drifts out the window

and chemistry attempts its Greek,
a capping of the peptic holes
to start the healing underneath

until the days prescribed are gone
and everything returns,
a minor twinge at first

and then
the steady hydrochlorics.
The stomach is a kind of life,

a widening in something longer,
a simple gourd, a metaphor,
a universe within itself.

The ulcers are its painful stars.

Three Akubras

Three Akubras in a row
my brothers underneath them
standing at the saleyards there
beside the auctioneer

a yard of vealers at the trot
the best there's been all morning
level-backed and well filled out
still glossy from the clover.

The auctioneer who sings them up
is lyrical about the grasses;
the buyers quietly pull an ear
or raise an eye to spotters.

What is it that they smile at now,
three brothers in a row?
The wildness of the auctioneer?
The quietness of the buyers?

Or is it just the years gone by
since first they saw the difference?
Or simply at the way the bids
rose freely through the ceiling?

Or are they smiling there at me
across the yard without Akubra
bemused by what I might have been
without my long refusal:

the ache all morning in the saddle
the branding irons, the cutting knife
stockbooks with insects late at night
the seasons of the ledger?

More likely it's the smile of three
who've kept it all together
the upstream and the downstream view
the tensions sensed and settled

as, suddenly, the hammer falls.
The vealers swirl out through the gate
away into the trucks and leave
the high tide of a market.

One smile under three Akubras ...
and perched there on the other side
of both a saleyard and a life
I wear a certain hatless pride.

The Phone

The centre of your
voice has gone
leaving just the
shattered edges.
Each night I hear it
on the phone
and see the turns of
tubes and fluids,
the plastic mask
across the nose,
transparent saddlebags
that drain you.
I hear in fragments
what has happened:
the injured disc,
the shallow lung
and golden staph
along the needle,
the half-stunned heart
that brought you in.
Not quite bad
enough to drive to
(a thousand Ks of
days and curves)
your children, minus
me, surround you.
And on the swell
of analgesics
you're drifting

with a last desire
as each night full of
stars and distance
I haul you back
along the wire.

Hay to Balranald

Heading west all afternoon the curvatures can still
    surprise you.
You might as well be out at sea; the skyline is a
    perfect circle.

Running the day's diagonal you're still a capsule at
    its core.
The afternoon is tilting upwards although a river near
    you slides

seaward in the same direction. The sun's arc is a
    further circle
setting through a streak of cirrus into the bitumen.

As in some floating telephoto semis slowly rush
    towards you
tall as tankers out to sea, their backwash spreading as
    they pass

a kind of violent sigh. All afternoon forgetting physics
you drive into the sky.

The Western Edge

1.

A long straight beach
leaves half the world.
The sea is full

but flat beneath an
unseen pressure.
Waves fold at their

final moment
below a roadway's
line of sight.

The evening here
is stippled slightly,
rippled by a kind of sigh.

The sun has just this moment gone.
The sea has found its
new enamel,

a richness in the skin —
orange, blue, but silver also ...
garish, yes, a cliché too,

but true as well
to certain moments
when something not

defined by science
is brimming high there
in your ribs,

a quiet expansion
of the tide,
and just this

subtlety of surface,
almost still
and wide with light.

2.
A day of
showers and sudden
sunlight, the wind

in gusts that rock the car
crosshatching now
the southwest corner,

the paddocks in their
winter flush,
the sheep a kind of punctuation

strung between the
stands of karri,
the vines bare wires

quiescent on the ridges,
a run of wines
across the tongue,

the echo of their names,
Leeuwin Estate, Cape Mentelle
and so many signposts

ending '-up',
Wilyabrup, Cowaramup,
a map which underlies the map,

deepening the texture —
as off there to the
west somewhere

and steadily all afternoon
a sun floats
to the scattered sea.

Miracles

The problem of evil
and man's free will,
the babies on the bayonets ...

God set it up
so long ago
intending it should all make sense.

The killers and their
free-will few
are dancing to an ancient law

and miracles
are just what happens
when God can't bear it any more.

Courtyard

Stillness in the
summer courtyard ...
all along the evening
the violet's coming down at last,
no movement in the leaves.

Your spouse has taken
in the plates
and left you silent here.
The immobility of leaves
translates into a fear

of what you know's
between the stars
and in the maple tree.
No wind and yet there's still a breath,
a kind of green unease.

This moment with the
finished wine
will be here when you're gone.
The horizontals of the leaves
do not bear thinking on.

The Wave

Sleeping on the western edge
the wind in squalls against the gutters
the surf a shudder

rising through the floor
I dream the stillness of my death
one wave arrested in its fall

and hardened into plastic,
the silence between stars.
And now this one

immeasurable moment
held for me and me alone
before the wave for you who hear it

collapses into sound.

The Signs

Half-dazed among the tilted shelves
of aubergines and apples, their skin
still clear with something she remembers,
before the days began to spin ...

The shine of fruit is all around her.
She cannot find the list she made.
Thursday, Friday, who knows which?
She can't remember if she's paid.

Olly thought it'd come to this
in those last months before he died —
embarrassment and love together
conspiring to keep her locked inside.

Why is it that they smile in passing,
nodding anonymously, yet using her name?
For a moment she's a kind of filmstar —
down at the market, dealing with fame.

'What was the name now?' she asks aloud.
'That nineteen thirties Metro star?'
As weighted down with plastic bags
she wonders where she left the car.

Belanglo

The murderer
who works among us
is sometimes vague
but not unlike us

brings his lunchbox
in each day
does not complain
about the pay

gets no memo
from the wife
has talked of bushwalks
once or twice

takes a sickie
now and then
but no more so
than other men

wears a name that
some forget
and others haven't
noticed yet

pulls up in a
4-wheel drive
there by nine and
gone at five

shows no anxiety
for promotion
absorbed no doubt
with one emotion

the nursing of a
slow contempt
the pleas, the shrieks,
the arguments

the rucksacks, knife,
adrenalin
the shallow graves
he sets them in

the dead now silent
in a smile
that doesn't yet
exist on file

the unseen, un-
accepting dead
who walk the fire trails
in his head

those moonlit gravels
white as bone ...
the killer that
we've always known

Reuben and Sarah
for H.S.

Reuben and Sarah
by God's good luck and desperation
more or less in equal parts

escape the fate of their relations
the small clear eyes of bureaucrats
the psychopaths who know their Bach

and swing around by sea
the belly of the world.
Far south, they work and wait it out

following the news
the great campaigns across the steppes
the storming into coastal fields

and young enough each night and aching
they dream the lists of Genesis
savouring the names.

But how could one
begin a child
and give it to the guns?

The relatives they see in dreams
by experts on the ways of trains
are herded into smoke.

And so they live
their long restraint
until one night, a southern August

alive with sirens, bells and shouts
a high surge in the street beside them
they know the tight blue

eyes are beaten
and finally the rising sun
and on a bed with frost outside

are free tonight
at last to bring
their children to this world.

The Secret
1954

There must have been a
day there somewhere,
some dawn with roosters,

undramatic,
a sentence spoken, something read,
when God had simply disappeared

and everything split off from that:
the sense of Christ out there in darkness,
personal, concerned

or held there in a grandson's smile
half-swinging on a door,
the Holy Spirit on its wings

snap-frozen above earth.
It might have been a saleyard Tuesday
by Thursday it was gone

with Sunday's sermon yet to come.
His wife, he saw, still had the gift,
his children, too, their lives went on

but always at a certain distance
as something, now remote to him,
each night absorbed their prayers.

His own were radiation only
fading into space.
So one day cracked, slipped back behind him

and more kept coming on
floating in their yellow dawns.
Matins, evensong, the confirmation class,

marriages and funerals,
the rhetoric still in the blood
although the heart had gone.

Once he would have tried to tell her
staring side by side from pillows
up towards the ceiling,

those first few words, 'you know, my dear …'
but that would now be ruination,
a double-barrelled

breach of trust.
And if not her then who else then?
The bishop at his cedar desk

polishing a pair of glasses
and staring at his shelves?
So one year more of

straitened silence
curved slowly through its feasts,
Advent, Christmas, Lent and Easter ...

His voice inside its concentration
had centres of its own
unknown to anyone but him

although the town's one self-declared
agnostic of the bars
smiled sometimes in the street.

And all that talk of doubt at college
thirty years before ...
of how with prayer and a concordance

all truth comes flooding back
filling up the space out there
stretched between the stars.

But that could not quite happen here
for God himself had left
this measure for externals only,

small decencies that would have flowed
from habit or respect.
He could perhaps declare himself

one Sunday in the pulpit
and walk out down the aisle between them
off into some meaner life

his wife there in the car beside him
sticking to her vows
as he would stick to his forever

although the Listener was gone.
So few among his words these days
wore any sort of weight.

His life, by now
three quarters gone,
would end, he knew,

with one old friend,
vicar from the town downriver,
talking of his colleague's faith

above a polished
box and husk
stalled between the pews.

And sometimes turning
through the gospels
he'd catch a scent of hell

enough at times
to shake his doubt.
Hell had no heat

nor vivid devils
chiselled into stone.
It was, he saw,

this glass enclosure
in which you lived
with shoulders bent ...

where nothing could be
truly said
or ever really meant.

The Relatives

And thus, when they see white people
suddenly appear in their country,
and settling themselves down to particular spots,
they imagine that they must have
formed an attachment for this land
in some other state of existence,
and hence conclude the settlers were at one period
black men, and their own relations.

Sir George Grey, 1841

The relatives with guns
have risen from the sea

rinsed by death and stripped of skin.
They stagger back along the valleys

bent beneath their fresh possessions.
The relatives with spears who greet them

smile strangely at their pale forgetting.
How is it that they miss a niece

and fail to see that ridge up there
is where Goanna Man went in?

Their speech, it seems,
is garbled by the waves,

their memory quite washed away.
Continuing as apparitions

they move along the valley floor,
securing in an ashen whiteness

the waterholes and easy flats
where wallabies come down at dusk.

It seems that they remember that.
And keep a musket handy.

The relatives who saw them land
are watching now from higher up

among dry rocks and trees.
Down there on the lower ground

the hard-eyed ghosts
have proved tenacious —

and have no wish to share.
And only far beyond this point

beyond the first exasperation
beyond the first exchange of blood

beyond the final ring of horsemen
closing in at dawn

will these relations from the sea
begin to feel in their amnesia

the first few basic verbs recur
or see beneath a strip of road

the contours of a hill once known
when hunted in bare feet;

and so will think increasingly
of those who moved among the trees

or faced them at a mountain's edge,
those relatives along the coasts

who welcomed back with disbelief
their cousins from the dead,

the relatives who rub like ghosts
against a line of late compassion

or stiffen in a cell.
The relatives who watched their kin

come rising from the waves
are walking back themselves from death.

And the sea continues on the sand
declaring its forgiveness.

The Squatters' Thesaurus

The frontier runs are cleared by language.
Myall niggers are *dispersed*.
The Bible and Charles Darwin both
declare the *sons of Cain* are cursed.

Two squatters on a front verandah
put their feet up to relax
and talk of last month's *dressing down*
or proper *thumping* of the blacks.

That lad of mine, one squatter smiles,
is much too keen on *rushing gins*.
We had a parson by last month
pronouncing on the *seven sins*.

Vigorous measures must be taken.
Outrages are up again.
Time, it seems, to be *doing the needful.*
They need a *dusting* now and then.

Bodies strewn about like saplings
are dragged into a pile and burnt.
The future talks of *settlement* ...
and murder is a language learnt.

Decalogue in Double Voice

But first, dear brethren, let me say
What brings a bishop out this way?
How pleased I am to speak to you
Words are many, blankets few
With everything so spic and span
Just like an English gentleman
The Ten Commandments are my text
What gubba nonsense coming next?
Especially from six to eight
Watch that stick and hook there, mate!
Number six 'Thou Shalt Not Kill'
My auntie's in the ground there still
Number seven's most important
Tells you what the white man oughtn't
'Thou Shalt Not Commit Adultery'
Unless she's black and velvety
'Thou Shalt Not Steal' is number eight
Or only dreaming any rate
Nine and ten we might defer
Thank you for the sermon, sir
Now let me see. Where should I start?
Number eight. I like that part.

The Second Law

Walking out at six in autumn
strolling through the red and gold
you catch the whiff of roast potatoes
floating on the early cold.

The sharpened air is rich with gravy,
the carbons of a passing car.
The time of day and time of year
combine to tell you what you are.

The evening star is up already
and in the branches very soon
as you turn in at your back door
will be the message of the moon.

The red meat and the trees are stained
with what is scattered at your feet.
The epic of your own five senses
is each day growing more complete.

The Boxes

The boxes
are a draughtsman's plan
with doorways in between;

the days and you
move quietly through them
equally at ease.

Then suddenly
as one half dies
your life becomes two rooms

which day by day
press in around you
making sure that soon

a two-room box
will be just one
inside a sunset home

with nurses
in the corridors
and tiredness in the bone.

And further on
there's one more still,
a long, lean sort of box

that has your measure-
ments exactly
and little need of locks.

Beyond the fire
there is one more
no bigger than your hand

to hold a body
which by then
will be a kind of sand,

a shellgrit which your
kids will take
beyond all need to care

and toss you from
the box at last
into the autumn air.

'Here's the money, Terry' *from* Guns

And, later, counting through the notes
the whole three thousand
done in hundreds

I'm wondering at their shallow blue,
the eyes, that is, that blinked just twice
and made their boyish sighting out the door.

The hair, of course, I'd seen before
dreaming at the racks,
the half-baked surfer's crazy mane.

What strikes me most is all those spaces
left between the words -
though 'Here's the money, Terry'

was spelt out plain enough.
With cash like that, of course, you'd throw
the ammo in for free —

but turning through the money now
there's just this flicker of a fear.
I dunno where you're headed, mate,

but don't the fuck start here.

Severance

Nice of you to
step in Henry,
need to have a
little word.
The section as
you know's downsizing,
got to shed
at least a third.

Yes, you thought
that you were needed
to make the whole
damn country work
but now we've found
it isn't true;
you're really a
redundant jerk

who thought your thirty
years with us
might somehow have
conferred the right
to think that you
could be of use.
In fact, you're just a
parasite

the government
cannot afford.

The budget now
is finely set.
User Pays and
Market Forces
are all the rhet-
oric you'll get.

You thought perhaps
there'd be a pension
indexed as a two-way bet?
And maybe some gold
watch or handshake
to settle an
outstanding debt?

Best you just
forget it, Henry.
There's your package
on the shelf ...
complimentary
Smith & Wesson.
Now step outside
and shoot yourself.

Brazilian Shoes

You like my new Brazilian shoes?
Each night they feature on the news

football fields of smoke and haze
ascend to let the leathers graze

before they scramble up a chute
to meditate their tan en route

towards the abattoirs and then
the molars and the soles of men.

The man who skins them gives his own
and likewise has a life on loan.

Death squads speak the kind of prose
that keeps machinists on their toes.

Sea lanes neatly intersect
and shoes are truths that don't connect

except when once or twice a week
you hear the silence in their shriek.

Timor mortis

Timor mortis
conturbat me
(as was it Horace said?)
which translates rather
roughly as
'I'm scared of being dead.'

How many rhymes
are we bequeathed
to resonate with 'breath'?
Six hundred years
of English verse
can offer only 'death'.

Our interest's more
in detail then,
that buffet of disease,
the epidemi-
ologies
that kill you by degrees.

You listen in your
midnight blood
for rumours up ahead
of what two doctors
might conclude
while signing you as dead.

Need a little
more on that?
'Don't worry,' says your mother.
'We're heart attacks
all down one side
and cancer down the other.'

The Waltz

Two couples walk a winter evening
half a block apart
the second brittle from the years
the first two at the start.

The two who follow have agreed
they cannot quite object
to what the girl is laughing at
when nuzzled on the neck.

She has a lovely, soaring squeal
and neither needs it said
that these are two requited lovers
not long out of bed.

Not even drunk the youngsters now
attempt a little dance —
as if this life might just allow
some kind of second chance

to all of us who stroll and smile
bemusedly behind —
if not for us then elsewhere in
the waltz of humankind

where laughter and a long frisson
from earlobe to the toes
bring back a world where once we all
went naked in our clothes.

The Chosen

Compassion is a minor island
Wearing at the edges.

Thousands just offshore are dying
Writhing in the waves

While just a few are washed ashore
Dazed upon the beaches

As one of us comes down the cliffs
To drag them from the sand

Scrape the small fish from their skin
Apply the special ointments.

When they are healed the rescued join us
Staring out to sea

Where each of us can recognise
A single language only

That salving code within a shriek
The lost cannot attempt.

Their tumult in the endless surf
Is heavy on the breeze

As one by one we stoop to save
The chosen on their knees.

Collateral Damage

Collateral damage, generals say ...
that summer when her parents split
and somehow she got lost between them

unwanted by the new recruits
bringing in their own;
Cinderella, just sixteen,

and sharing with a brother
the ATM and plastic magic
while dad is overseas;

her stripping it as quiet revenge,
the blow-in of the youthful drunks,
the advent of the pushers

as schoolwork now becomes a habit
running up her arm
and everything is loans and lies.

The boyfriend proves a user too.
She dabbles at the edge of sleaze
but lasts a few nights only;

does some running for the dealers
closer to the source,
inscrutables from Cabramatta

who'd never use a fit themselves
but chase the dragon only.
Every day she's got to have it;

drains each parent, makes them pay
but cannot crack their
perfect circles;

her stories grow
each week more wild
but not unlike the truth —

AIDS syringes at the neck,
hostage in a car.
And always, somewhere, deeper down

the ache of her nostalgia:
those summers back before the split
when everything was high blue sky

and still no touch of difference on her
when siblings strolled up from the beach
hosed the sand from off their feet

and all sat down to lunch,
her father with a Tooheys open
her mother at the bench.

Six months, twelve,
maybe eighteen
she's disappearing by degrees

into her own mythology,
the jobs that strangely fade away,
the dole that always goes to dealers,

her battles with the clerks.
But now, today, her father's rung
to ask her to the beach for Christmas

and here tonight in this last house
to offer her some passing shelter
she's saying like a happy child

Make sure you wake me up, OK?
My dad'll be here right on nine.
Trying out a smile.

My Mother's Letters

I have my mother's letters
in a Woolworths plastic bag,
three or four, to be precise,

five decades worth of admonitions,
her longhand all around the type
with, now and then, some Pitman script

learned when she was twenty.
I don't destroy them ... or re-read them.
Their arguments go round and round,

the tone so much *now then, my boy*,
and *don't you kid yourself*
they float like gunsmoke in a cupboard

down there where I keep my shoes.
Genes and history, politicians,
the harshness of a mother's maxims,

they swirl there like the upper boughs
of two tall family trees.
To quote from them verbatim

would be indelicate.
Some evening I, inevitably,
or someone else, my son perhaps,

will toss them in a bin on wheels
or quietly light a match.
That day, I hope, is some years out.

Silently in bags meanwhile
her fifty years' advice and love
are patient in their plastic.

The Homestead

High above the Clarence now
I'm talking on this tall verandah,
heirloom of my brother's.

It looks out on the downstream view
hazed and deepened with September,
this scattering of burn-off fires —

the blues, the browns, the greens, the greys
unified by smoke —
as are the levels of the air,

the levels of the river.
I have to tell myself, first-born,
why none of this is mine:

the sweat, the boredom and the bank,
the entropy of fences,
the tiredness in the bones at evening,

the branding iron, the cutting knives,
the squalling calves and moaning mothers,
the auctioneer's uneven song,

the cowshit shindeep in the crushes ...
the murmur too I caught much later
of Bundjalung millennia,

the peoples of the river
whose voices now I still can hear
sometimes on a telephone,

more often in the rapids.
Two days' driving to the south
I have a first-floor slice of air

and cut to other mountains.
Eighty-three square metres neat
complete my acreage —

nothing extra to requirement.
Why is it then things don't add up?
Half pain, half pleasure, half relief

and something in the eye's delight.
Why is it that I still return?
Why is it that I need to have

my ashes in the river?

The Lid

The story keeps on coming back,
a man my father knew,
that grazier across the river
up north a mile or two,

a story that my father spun
to last me all my life
of how a man should not behave
when burying a wife.

All through the funeral he'd wept ...
the priest there going on
about St Peter and the gates
through which his wife had gone.

His sobbing at the grave, Dad found,
was harder still to bear.
The men in suits, the women in
the best they had to wear

knew deeper down it couldn't pass,
no matter *who* had died.
Extravagance like this was always
better kept inside.

At last the man who sent his beasts
to die on Tuesdays gave
one final, high unseemly cry
and leapt into the grave.

'Mate,' he yelled. 'Don't go. Don't go!'
And scrabbled at the wood.
A friend reached in to fish him out
as any Christian would.

The women in their hats stood back.
Two men jumped in the trench
and skidding on the polished lid
contrived at last to wrench

him out and lead him to his car.
The clergyman intoned
'Ashes to ashes, dust to dust'.
They heard the broken moans

coming from a side window.
He hammered at the wheel.
'Mate, he yelled. 'Don't leave me mate.'
Not knowing what to feel,

the mourners now were drifting off
towards their dusty cars.
My father always finished here
as if he'd gone too far.

But I could hear the slamming doors,
the hearse without much chrome
and dual decisions made to miss
the wake and head straight home.

'Mate, oh mate!' the man had cried,
releasing all their fears.
The sound of boots on coffin wood
survives them down the years.

The Heart is Like a Lazy Lizard

for Alison

1.

The heart is like a lazy lizard
looking for the sun,
waiting for a touch of spring
before it starts to run.

2.

Love's a drunken butterfly
tilting through the flowers.
For some it lingers forty years;
for others, forty hours.

3.

The heart is also Eden's snake
flickering its tongue —
eyeing off the not-so-old ...
and those no-longer-young.

4.

Love is just a roadside crow
flattened in the sun,
the kind of accident that might
occur to anyone.

5.

By day the heart's a sturdy pump
chugging at the flow.
By night it talks in metaphors
of what we hardly know.

Reflecting on the Mortals

Now that science
has banished death
I like to spend an afternoon

reflecting on the mortals.
My great grandfather was, I think,
the last to die of cancer,

his wife the final stroke but three.
It must have been a bit chaotic
there before the end,

so near and yet so far.
The future yawns before us now,
a mountain panorama

whose edge cannot exist.
A hurriedness is what survives them,
those mortals in their books.

Each day we find it slightly harder
quite to understand,
to catch and hold that sense with which

they'd lie on starry nights
and stare into the sky,
hearing the star-stuff in their heart,

the numbers in its beating.
They liked the thought of meteors.
Such things, for us, are mere detritus,

the operation of old laws
that we have more or less transcended.
We have, of course, the mortals' music

tied so firmly into time
yet striving to break free;
we sense its exaltation

though less and less each year, it's true.
Accidents can still occur.
And now and then, increasingly,

we hear that someone has declined
the dictates of infinity
and quietly pressed a switch.

Mortals too accomplished this
but in a different way.
Jumping the queue, it's said they called it,

shortening the ration.
We immortals, saved by science,
stroll slowly on forever.

The afternoons are afternoons
although from time to time
we have to shift our suns like nomads.

The mortals called this heaven.

Credo

The dark-night-of-the-soul agnostic
prefers the right to doubt.
The world's too much beset by those
who know what they're about.

The dark-night-of-the-soul agnostic
says 'yes, maybe … although'.
He has his own utopias
but would like you to know

that in a year or so he might
prefer another view —
and even all his sceptic's faith
could one day vanish too

but this, he's fairly sure, would fade
and doubt come back once more.
The dark-night-of-the-soul agnostic
does not besiege your door.

He builds no temple out of bricks
and does not like to preach.
He thinks conviction more impressive
slightly out of reach.

Jane's Story

My friend Jane the clergywoman
slender as a silver birch
loves to tell the story of
her first time at a country church

and how the guy who tolled the bell
was out of town or in poor health
and how in all her priestly gear
she'd had to man the rope herself

the knot high there above her head
its fibre hefty as the tone
of that high single bell above her
set to ring at fourteen stone

the normal sexton's weight-on-scale
a measure of his noble girth
and how he'd ring all thirty-three
years that Christ has spent on earth

and how such ringing lifted her
that many times above the ground
soaring high as if to heaven
then parachuting gently down.

The ways of Christ would not be easy
she saw while flailing through the air
clinging to that godly stockwhip
cracking in the belfry there

until, all done, she smoothed her robes
and strolled inside to pray and preach.
Red-faced as the wine she held
she gave Christ's body each to each.

Sermon

Those of you
who leave your trace
on stone, on paper or in air

will soon exist
by such marks only
and just for those who find they care.

These marks will not tell
who you were
nor what the ceiling said at four.

Those who later
praise the traces
will not have known you at the core.

Nor even will your
closest friends
strolling at the edge of life;

their knowledge is
at best a guess —
as is the husband's or the wife's.

The marks you make
become yourselves,
eventually the truer part.

The world is littered
with the husks
of those who vanished into art.

The memories
we leave the living
are likewise fictions more or less.

The messages
all run one way.
No one knows your true address.

Tango

How is it that such solid couples
dance a tango in the mind,
these lovers who have never danced
and time has lovingly refined?

They've grown to fit each other's shape;
they've almost nothing to regret.
The rhythm struts with the recall
of all the risks not taken yet —

the not-quite-youthful sad affair
warm with failure from the start.
Decades and the bandoneon
transmute them to a dancer's art

which promises in every pass
the languorous delays of sex,
a love like hands beneath the clothes
and moonlit, reminiscent decks

of voyages they will never dance on,
the places they will never see.
Nostalgia for the not-quite-tried?
What is it that has set them free?

Adulterers

After that first urgent
kissing at the door
and all the prearrangements

whispered down the phone
and all that splendid
disarray of clothes,

the interplay of skins and liquids,
that short delirium of smells
and all such pure

antiphonal delights
the cigarettes are lit at last ...
and sprawled there in a

twist of sweat
a conversation comes to life:
obsessions of the absent husband,

shortfalls of the absent wife.

The Recipe

'A sonnnet tells me nothing but itself',
as William Carlos Williams liked to say —
somewhat perversely lifting from the shelf
a pattern even free verse must obey.
Your sonnet's eight and six are sacrosanct;
the greatest chef would hardly dare to alter
the ancient taste for eight lines neatly ranked —
then six from what Italians call the *volta*.
A rhyme scheme down the side is *de rigueur*,
Elizabethan maybe — or Petrarchan.
And cooks from Spenser on will all concur
the sonnet is the dish to make your mark in.
By God, we're there and, yes, you're doing fine.
And now, like pepper, add the fourteenth line.

The Visit

She's done the settlement at last;
Her husband now is on his way —
When suddenly the plot's more complex.
Mother has arrived to stay.

Not just the normal cheering up
Or checking out the children's tricks.
At eighty-four she's 'got a man',
Still vertical at eighty-six.

They want the double bed, it seems,
Although they've yet to 'tie the knot'.
The daughter is a little miffed
But settles for a lesser spot.

Mum and boyfriend after lunch
Decide to have a 'quick lie down'.
The daughter at the kitchen sink
Cannot quite undo her frown.

Unbearably, they're standing there
Ready for a friendly clutch.
'Don't worry,' whispers mother, winking.
'He doesn't quite get up to much.'

Of all the small humiliations
Life bestows before you're dead
The greatest is your mother and
Her boyfriend in your double bed.

Or that is what the daughter thinks
Staring at the spare room ceiling —
As down the hall she hears their voices
And her bed, fill up with feeling.

The Poem That You Haven't Seen

The poem that you haven't seen
and someone should by now have written

concerns the sub K219
holed and damaged off Bermuda,

its death chutes locked on Washington
New York and Boston, its power plant sliding

into meltdown. It tells of how
with no remote, two Russians wound

all four reactor rods to safety.
The poem that you haven't seen

revives how Sergei Preminin,
apprentice seaman, just on twenty,

and First Lieutenant Belikov
between them in that cancelled air

cranked by hand the death rods down
through 65 degrees of heat

wreathed with gas and radiation.
The poem tells of how the first

and then the other man passed out
and in his turn was dragged aside

and how Sergei went stumbling back
to fix the rod that saved the cities

and how the exit hatch slammed shut
and how the captain heard that death

gasping on the intercom.
The poem that has not been written

would also show the less dramatic
efforts made to tow and salvage

before the submarine in silence
sank slowly through 6,000 metres.

The poem that has not been written
restores to us the morning traffic

in Washington, New York and Boston
and has a grab of Gorbachev

with Reagan stooped at Reykjavik
five days later over papers.

The poem that has not been written
ends with Sergei Preminin —

and the sub K219
corroding on the ocean floor,

its missiles undelivered.

Monaro

i. m. Rosalie Gascoigne

Sawn up out of
soft drink crates
it has the yellowness

of summer,
that blondness David
Campbell spoke of,

the blackness of a
vanished language
illegibly cut into parts

and shifted into
ridges, valleys,
a texturing of

scrappy trees.
The weathered paint
is more a stain,

the colour of an
early morning,
those first few level

rays of sun
before the dew
begins to rise.

And as she knocks it
all together
painfully

from all its parts
she's made the jump
all poets make:

a simile of soft drink
boxes
scattered in a yard,

that yellow
metaphor of hills
rolling to the east of Cooma.

The Sky

'All poetry,' says Ashbery
'is basically about the weather.'
And paying for a view at last

I find that I agree.
I like to watch it blowing in,
the stateliness of clouds through glass.

I like to see the shift of showers
sideways through the postcodes,
the way they bump against the hills.

Connoisseur of mountain haze,
I watch the blues of smoke or mist
out there on the ranges.

Also the indigos of dusk,
the violets dropping off the spectrum,
the streetlights coming on.

Some people like to feel the soil
dissolve between their fingers,
the flowers it might,

with care, supply.
My balcony's low maintenance.
I cultivate the sky.

Melons
for Alison

Lost in a field of
friendly melons

tossed in a vat of
thickened cream

licked by a thousand
fervent puppies

that was the substance
of my dream.

Did it really
howl and happen

somewhere in this
moonlit bed?

So many circles
of confusion

whirling in my
hapless head.

Did I dream
or was I there?

What acres were we
really in?

As now next morning
writing this

I smell the melons
on my skin.

Dogs and God

That bikie with his
girl as pillion,
that kelpie in his

sidecar there
singing in the wind ...
The girl with blonde hair

blowing back
is smiling sidelong
at the dog

who measures in his
cancelled song
the richness of the instant ...

And who among you
cruising by
would still deny

the fact of heaven?
If dogs have souls
and God's tattooed

and every angel
has blonde hair
streaming from a helmet ...

Algebra

1.
The way we shuffle pillowtalk
With what our xs did

And how they're at a flywire door
Taking back the kid

2.
The way an x's memory dries
Like liquid on the skin

The way they are a souvenir
You can't put in the bin

3.
Two xs over cappuccinos
Civilized at last

See how they almost never touch
Too tender from the past

4.
Here now on the courthouse steps
The sky becomes less mean

Though each one's certain they alone
Have had the full dryclean

5.
Two *x*s and their grown-up kids
The nature / nurture ploy

Which one of them can claim the girl?
And which one spoilt the boy?

6.
Although all *x*s thin like smoke
Their names may be confused

Across a table or in bed
A wrong endearment used

7.
Normally but not always
The in-laws fade because

They seem more certain than the *x*
Whose fault it really was

8.
When wedding bells are wiped away
The blackboard leaves an image

2 x *x* + 1 + 2
The algebra of marriage

9.

Some xs drop right off the world
And go to be alone

While others live by email or
The lilting of a phone

10.

It seems that xs never leave
As old friends misaddress

The envelope of their goodwill
Your y is called an x

11.

On seeing xs there are those
You'd cross the road to greet

And those for whom you wouldn't risk
The traffic in the street.

12.

Do xs lose the pheromones
That waft between the sexes?

Some moments in a restaurant
Will always be an x's

13.

Two *x*s in a coffee bar
Give hope for Palestine

Who pays this time, who pays next
A kind of Auld Lang Syne

14.

And finally the day arrives
When neither can agree

On who dropped whom and why — and who's
The dumper or dumpee?

15.

You're probably an *x* yourself
Statistics say it's so

Some Year 10 sweethearts last until
The fire says who's to go

16.

Deaths are different — often less
Ambiguous — or more

No chances of rapprochement and
No shouting at the door

17.

Virgins do not yet have xs
Their time is yet to come

xs add complexity
Intensify the sum

18.

Most equations have an x
Or y and z as well

The Goddess of the Second Chance
Still has us in her spell

Twenty Fingers

for Alison & Kaye

Together they are playing now
Though forty years have passed.
They are again two twelve-year-olds
And still a fraction fast.

The duet piece that moved their mums
And quietly charmed their friends
Is called 'Sleigh Bells' and harnessed up
To canter round the bends.

One husband each has toppled off;
They've had six kids all told.
Forty years the sleigh bells ring —
But they are twelve years old.

Twenty fingers find the notes
And two new men appear.
Life's grown rich with counterpoint
Year by vanished year.

A double stave of memory
Has sat them down together.
Two young girls of fifty-four
Play against the weather.

The Open Field

Now, on the other side of sixty,
you're like an open field.
Soon the disabilities

will start to sprinkle down,
those fancy Greek and Latin tags.
The same low isobars will bring

the illnesses as well,
that list of diminutions:
the bloodstream, once a freeway

is now a *cul de sac*;
the heart taps out its hapless morse;
a great metropolis of nerves

is slowly frozen over
and cancers, *sotto voce*, make
their covenants of pain.

When clouds like these hang overhead
you know you're just an open field
waiting for the rain.

The Revelation

The revelation came from space,
a stray star swinging low and loose;
wise men, camels and a virgin,
angels, oxen, straw,
soldiers, zealots, slippery priests,
an empire at its sharpened edge,
the promise of a death built in
immutable as logic.
It had the taste of desert, too;
distractions rippled in the sand.
The destiny it wore within
would bear no variation.
Starting out from shepherd's talk,
it vanished in translation.

The Sparrows at Brunetti's

The sparrows at Brunetti's
define the word 'alert'
perching on vacated chairs,
pesky, preened and pert.

The remnants they have cornered
have fine Italian names.
Before a blonde in black can swoop
they've measured out their claims.

Among spent cappuccinos
and empty latte glasses,
the sparrows' feel for real estate
defeats the middle classes.

Each bird has long developed
a rich, pragmatic taste:
they recognise a *crema* — and
there's nothing goes to waste.

As perky *cognoscenti*
they've found their final niche —
on Faraday with students and
a slice of *nouveau riche*.

The treble of their flutter
makes the day complete.
Edgy as the traffic, they're
the caffeine in the street.

Grafton, 1946

for Robert Gray

A Clarence mist on lower reaches
and Jerseys after milking;
morning shadows crawling back
beneath the jacarandas;

the dented shine of milk cans too
waiting for the lorry
and butter factories with their names
already lost to rain ...

which makes it 1946,
a booth in Langley's Café,
chocolate malted, toasted sandwich,
tomatoes moist with sun

and Kraft cheese from a packet flattened
between two sheets of bread,
salted, peppered, pressed and seared,
like poems to be written.

Men with empty sleeves elicit
whispered explanations.
My parents, in their early thirties,
quietly milk their tea.

Most graziers have been 'Reserved',
breeding beef for diggers.
The roar inside the RSL
will always be off-limits.

The Bride is Flying

for Rosemary Laing

The bride is flying,
1910,
her gown a kind of parachute

though done with full-length sleeves;
her veil, we see, already gone
to flaunt her long black hair.

The whiteness of her wedding dress
is like a cloud above the cliffs.
Inside a dream, or out of it,

she's learning how to fly.
Her innocence is trousseau linen
yet to bear a stain.

Her panorama's thick with risk,
a husband with cigar and whisky
laughing at the club

and children in a bloody queue
swimming in the amniotic
as she is now in air

high above the scarp and forest.
She almost has the knack of it,
correcting as she goes.

A White Beach to Dance on

One after one, they have
checked out, the bastards:
the unwedded mother who
put on to me
the stuff that she suffered
each day in the street;
the stepfathers grunting
by turn in my ear
as if I was only a
cushion with holes,
me watching their
faces turn red;
the husband I fled to
as soon as I could,
who knocked me up first
in a couple of weeks
then knocked me down
cold on the floor;
the bastard who'd do it
only when drunk
and never take
no for an answer;
the bastard who'd beat up his
own flesh and blood
whenever they
showed any spirit;
the husband I slept with for
thirty-five years,
him who I finally

fled from for good,
him with his
fridge full of beer.
They're dead, they're all dead,
like birds off a branch,
they're shellgrit or
shit in a hole.
I've outlived the lot
and so wriggled free.
They've left me ten years
to use as I choose,
a chance to find friends
who'll say what they see,
a white beach to dance on
as well as I can,
and think of forgiveness,
a little, maybe;
then waltz off the
edge of the world.

The Cello Sonatas of J.S. Bach

are made of passages and stairways,
halls that do not have an ending,
stairs with landings halfway up

to show the sudden stars.
The architect loves repetition ...
with secret variations

you don't quite see at first:
doorways in a long perspective
that actually grow smaller;

windows in a night façade
with slightly different sills.
They have an amplitude as well

to match the cello's belly,
curlicues and subtle serifs
echoing the scroll.

The scratchy record by Casals,
inscribed on bakelite,
is still so far the best of Bach.

Play it late, say 3 a.m.,
and like some wild, forgotten child
you'll run all night the empty stairwells

flowering in the dark.

Huntsman

To make a sonnet is the same
as cutting off a huntsman's legs
to fit into a box, a game ...
wherein you wield the scissors' edge

to nip off what will not quite fit.
You hear that aria of pain
the spider sings at every snip —
eight legs, eight lines to fit the frame.

But not, my student says to me,
if art starts off inside the box,
each leg to its extremity
the way that feet fit into socks.

And yet, I say, the spider dreams
that life is not quite what it seems.

I Think I Could Turn Awhile

1.

I think I could turn awhile and write like the Americans,
they are so at ease in their syllables, irregular as eyelids,
various as the sea.
They do not hear the iamb ticking, tetchy with its small demands.
Their pronouns are huger than Texas.
I too would find my metaphysics
as I sliced my sedan through a long prairie night.
The turkey sheds of Minnesota, the slanted dusk of Iowa,
the breakers on the Big Sur coast and the stillness in the Rockies
would each be a part of my redemption.
I too would be an heir of Whitman
despite all his curious shyness with women.
I'd rummage through his catalogues, those holy repetitions,
hearing the King James Bible singing
through cirrus the size of all the eastern states
drifting by splendidly over my head.

2.

But somehow after
half a book
I know that I
would then turn back.
That rhetoric is
someone else's;
it works with very
different vowels.
I'd hear the clipped
iambics calling,

my template just
below the line.
I'd feel the need for
tighter turns,
a tiredness with the
larger flourish,
their drumroll of a
flag unfurled.
'That would be good,'
as Frost surmised,
'both going and coming back',
back to something
leaner, drier,
back to something
lower-key:
the chicken sheds of
Wallabadah ...
a summer on the
Clarence maybe ...

'Down with Beauty!' 'Long Live Death!'

'Down with Beauty!' 'Long Live Death!'
Two gods share a single breath.

Their warriors can all agree
on how to circumscribe the free

and are themselves in turn confined
by being of the same small mind.

A Muslim and a Catholic phrase
may equally distress our days;

the latter from the Spanish war,
the former sure the hip's a whore.

'Down with Beauty!' 'Down with Life!'
All throats are naked to the knife.

As holy men sweep up the dead
their two gods shake a single head.

The Stalinists, the Taliban

In dreams they give you lines each night,
the Stalinists, the Taliban,
in trench coats or in holy white.
So, too, the mullahs of Iran.
The SS men of Hitler's packs
and Torquemada's Inquisition
with jackboots or with stretching racks
assist you reaching a decision.
The judge from Salem sees you as a
devil he's unmasked at last;
the imam in his sour madrassa
wrings your future from his past.
The certain like their sonnets neat.
And need your screams to be complete.

A Short History of Immigration

'Ohl my God!' say the Eora.
'What's all that red / white / blue?'
'Oh, my God!' says Captain Phillip.
'We've brought the Irish too.'

'Oh, my God!' say London lags.
'Please send us no more thieves.'
'Begorrah, Lord!' the Irish say.
'Be sparin' us Chinese!'

'Bloody hell, send back Kanakas!'
our noble workers jeer.
'They cut the cane in half the time.
A man can't buy a beer.'

'Dear God of England' Barton prays,
'do keep our country white …
and leave the heathen in his place
far north and out of sight.'

'Oh, King of Jazz' the twenties roar.
'It's Populate or Perish!
A country white as Reckitt's Blue's
the only one to cherish.'

'God help us quick' says '42,
'We're damn well on our knees.
The Peril's here. Bring on the Yanks
to paste the Japanese.'

'And look, dear God, here come the Dagoes
bouncing off the boat.
We're nearly out of Dutch and Danes ...
and Englishmen of note.'

'And now, dear God, here come the Balts
escaping Mother Russia.
Next week we'll have the Reds as well,
Ivan and Natasha.'

'Oh, my God,' the Balts exclaim —
and Dagoes with degrees.
'What's this the tide is throwing up,
the bloody Vietnamese?

We'll all be strangled in our sleep
and take to heroin.
You hardly know which vault these days
to keep your money in.'

'Oh, my God!' we shriek as one.
'Here come the men in scarves.
They bang their head against the floor.
They don't do things by halves.'

'Let them join the queue,' we say,
'wherever it might be —
and let them have their backside stamped
before they put to sea.

He who flees a terrorist
is prob'ly one himself.
The way of true compassion is ...
to send them somewhere else,

some atoll where, in time, the tide
will rise by twenty metres.
A logical solution, yes?
Could anything be neater?

The advent of such dodgy types
will make us all the poorer.'
'By Christ, you know, you might be right,'
declares an old Eora.

Eora: Aboriginal people around Sydney.

Arthur Phillip

Why is it dreams are like our history,
two parts pride and two parts shame?
First in the world with secret ballot,
slow to give murder a working name.

Can it be we're still a dream
disrupting Arthur Phillip's sleep?
Inside that eighteenth century head
we're convicts, whipped, who will not weep

or 'Native Aboriginees'
too primal to salute the king
who greets us all with half a wave
and hopes that we're not suffering.

Transported dreams bestowed the vote
and, later, all that kings can give —
but stories done with guns and flags
are where we find we still must live.

Nineteen one

Why do I keep on seeing this?
New Year's morning, nineteen one,
six a.m., the river calm.

A light mist ribbons coastal steamers
hawsered at a timber wharf
high up in New South Wales,

the Clarence or the Richmond, maybe.
There's a whiff of beer and sawdust.
a tang of horse manure.

The windows are in one foot segments,
offering their smaller views.
A few men are about already,

each one with his hat or cap.
The stillness in the river now
is almost absolute;

the layers of the mist declare it.
The morning light is sourceless
though slanted from the east —

as now a century begins ...
a rattling of kegs and cans,
the clip-and-clop of horses

and wheel rims grinding gravel.
But mainly it's this misty calm —
and how, while rising from their beds

with all those curlicues of brass,
so few of them are troubled by
the weight of what's to come.

2001

We will decide
Who comes to this country —
And the circumstances
In which they come.

How like a piece of poetry it was,
the roughening iambics,
those sharpened cs, like angled pikes,

the two-beat lines that got us going —
except line 3 which had its extra
fist banged on the table.

Note the subtle half rhyme too,
'country' matched with 'come'
and how the preposition 'in'

assumes its proper place.
Like most great poetry, of course,
it's mainly made from echoes:

the glorious Three Hundred Greeks
who held Thermopylae
and Winston Churchill roaring still

'We shall fight them on the beaches ...'
Like all such deathless works of art
it's shivering with myth:

the golden hordes who spoiled our sleep
across two centuries;
the bard far back with lyre and smoke

declaiming his alliterations;
the ancient battles of his race
with dragons, gods and men.

No wonder, then, that those who might
have shown us something else,
defeated now by poetry,

had nowhere left to turn.

The Book of his Addresses

The book of his addresses
is like the mind of God,

older than he'd like,
with some names down the bottom

seriously frayed.
Too many of its entries

have had a line drawn through —
and so he keeps on losing

the argument with death.
The entropy of God,

it's clear, is heaven-sent.
Drawing near the silence,

the book of his addresses
becomes more eloquent.

Paddock of the Saved
for Coral Hull

You mentioned it just once —
and somehow I've remembered
your paddock of the saved;

how you bought them up at sales,
scrawny bullocks, old dry cows,
saved them from a fate in tins,

saved them from the final concrete,
the shit, the fear, the hammer-gun.
The auctioneer is smiling;

the trucker shares the joke
but drops them (like an angel) at
your cattle-ramp to heaven.

I see them fanning out,
knowing they've been rescued
but not quite sure from what.

The days, the weeks, the months go by;
the feed is green, then brown,
a ragged, undistinguished paddock,

lightly timbered with a creek
that never quite goes dry.
The barks of dogs are not in close-up;

no more stockmen, no more whips.
Subject to the weather only,
they're relishing the alternations

of sun with drifting cloud —
until, at last, they feel a stiffness
they'd never quite expected.

You check them every month or so;
truck in hay when times are tough.
They die, in turn, *au naturel*,

front feet down and then the back,
collapsing from the years.
You get the vet to see them off

if nothing can be done.
When all the rest are protein only
flowing to the knives

you save this dozen steers and cows
to live their slow, symbolic lives
and die from other causes —

not so unlike those men with sticks
ten thousand years ago
who offered them

the covenant of grassed enclosures
and talked in secret voices that
they still don't understand.

The Smile

One thinks of those forgotten names
so smugly famous in their time,
masters of the parlour games
as well as of the tricks of rhyme.

They smile at their presumptive power,
Robert Santry, Stirton Giles,
heroes of the day and hour,
masters of the minor styles

that tell you, yes, that spring will bloom
that God is in his highest heaven
that chancellors will bring no gloom
that dinner must be served at seven.

Such poets rarely die of poxes;
they are extravagantly mourned
then shouldered off in shining boxes
and given tombstones, much-adorned.

Oblivion now sets the pace
and ushers in the newer style.
Cheeks, in weeks, rot off the face
but nothing can destroy the smile.

Out There

The stars out there between the towns
reach right down to the edges —
or hang as if thrown up by chance
and casually tethered.

It's 'bible-black'-except for them.
There won't be any moon.
They're floating there like funeral flowers
across a dark lagoon.

I have no wish to count them off
or be their registrar.
I've seen what's out there way beyond
the city lights and cars

that flow like complex sentences
too difficult to parse.
I love the carbon compromise,
the smell of coffee bars.

Reef

In all the glory of Linnaeus,
they're swimming in their free verse world.
They're like some catalogue of Whitman's,
a triumph of the wide demotic:
the angelfish, the damselfish
and every sort of wrasse,
the surgeonfish, the triggerfish,
the flutemouths, snappers, fusiliers,
the cardinals, the goatfish,
the Bennett's butterfly,
in widescreen and in technicolor
through every tremor of the spectrum;
the filefish and the parrotfish,
the clownfish with their whites and orange.
In all the reefs that still survive:
the pufferfish, the barracuda,
the jawfish on the bottom,
the anglerfish, the frogfish
in all their gothic splendour;
the seahorse, too, dealt straight from myth,
the hawkfish, gophies and the blennies,
the burrfish known as spiny puffer ...
I saw them once, a small selection.
Unschooled in any Latin,
they swam beyond nomenclature,
rejoicing in their names.

Lethe

A vacant face is in the hallway,
one I've not been told about.

It stares at my agnostic soul
as if it doubts my right to doubt.

I keep on talking to my hostess
and try to find the thread again.

She tells me it's dementia,
her mother's not in any pain.

Even so, the pain is there —
if not the mother's, then the daughter's.

We're standing here like ancient Greeks
gathered at the final water.

Some Nights
for Kevin Hart

Some nights I envy God his poets,
their metaphors of cloud and moon,
their crises of the soul,

the way each tree, each stone, each pool
is never just itself.
Disinclined to find a term

like 'grace' in my thesaurus,
I will admit, when close to dawn,
a whiteness in between the words,

a grammar deeper than the signs
through which we're meant to sense it.
The stars though, still, are what I need —

their different rates of dying,
the way their light survives them.
How is it that a jumbo jet

can lumber into air?
Why is it that they're not enough,
the mysteries of physics?

Dancing by the Sea

1.

Peace and Justice,
abstract nouns,
were meant to be together.
Transparent and
opaque by turn,
they love the salty weather.

How far back
does Justice go
and whose turn is it now?
The brawling boys
are in a queue —
the only question's how

the local lad
will polish up
to ask her for a dance.
She's delicate,
hard-pressed and rare;
he'll have to take his chance

for both sharp sides
of Justice must
be honoured — then forgotten
as Peace, while waltzing
round the room,
wears only flimsy cotton.

And so our pair of
abstract nouns,
is dancing by the sea.
In bed together
afterwards
they dream of you and me.

2.
The sweat dries on
their bodies and
they're languorously spent.
'I shouldn't tell you
but,' she yawns,
'you've lost the argument.

Waving guns
and gods and flags
can never be the answer.
No girl will ever
sleep with those,
however smooth the dancer.'

Young Justice doesn't
quite know how
he got her into bed.
Who was it who
was following?
And who was it who led?

The boys back home
may spill their beer
and say he's sold them out

but, now that he
has slept with Peace,
he knows what life's about.

Their future may not
last the summer;
they have no guarantee.
A moon, though, pales
their bodies and
a breeze blows off the sea.

Heaven

When their snipers kill one of us
we go to heaven as martyrs;
when we kill them they go to hell.

Abu Othman, Iraqi Sniper, 2005

Extra ecclesiam nulla salus (There is no salvation outside the church]
Cyprian of Carthage

1.

The infidels are roasting elsewhere;
their smell is sweet to heaven.

All outside the church will burn …
including that Iraqi sniper

who praises God each time he kills —
his victims drop straight through to hell.

High there in his minaret
he's just a shellburst short of heaven.

2.

The poetry of
fear and loathing,
how long's it been around?

Between what once were
Eden's rivers
it's on the mobile phone:

the panicked rifle
slanting down,
the man still on the floor,

the rhythm, the alliteration:
fucking faking, fucking faking —
and then the poet, under pressure,

trying it the other way —
faking fucking, faking fucking
as now one shot resolves it.

Well, he's dead now —
the poem not quite
finished somehow.

3.
What's his sacred elevation,
this martyr in his rage —
as, courtesy a robot crane,
he's hauled away offstage?

Is he halfway up to heaven?
Is he almost there?
Does Allah's hand reach down to him
across the savage air?

Will all those promises be kept?
Is there some further test?
Does Allah want the half blown-up
who failed but did their best?

Waking later with the wounded,
the chaos of their sounds,
his soul is one small fleck of debris
floating slowly down.

4.
We need the gods
to raise the green
when winter's almost done.

We need the gods
to guarantee
spring's tilt towards the sun.

We need the gods
to teach us how
to recognise the cruel

and help with our
rapprochements when
our tempers start to cool.

We need the gods
to promise that
we never really die,

that some essential
part of us
will soar into the sky.

We need the gods
to tell us what
we're certain they would say,

how heretics
and infidels
must burn if they should stray.

We need them, too,
beside us as
our breath is thinning out.

I love the sad,
agnostic god
who taught me how to doubt.

Author's Note

These poems are drawn from more than forty years of writing. As well as reflecting my personal preferences, the selections have been influenced by responses at public readings, inclusions in anthologies and by comments offered by valued friends, colleagues and readers. I have chosen (with one exception) to leave the poems as they were first published rather than revising them. My five verse novels, my tandem translations and my eight-liner travel chapbooks are not sampled here and are, in most cases, still available elsewhere.

Acknowledgements

Thanks are due to the editors of the magazines, newspapers and anthologies where these poems first appeared or reappeared. I would also thank the succession of enterprising and committed publishers of my poetry collections over forty years. I would also like to thank Susan Somerville, Carolyn Mau and my partner, Alison Hastie, for their forbearance and encouragement at successive times over the decades.

Colleagues such as Alan Gould, John Foulcher, Roger McDonald and Adrian Caesar and several others also provided valuable advice when it was sought.

Thanks are also due to ADFA, University of New South Wales, where I have been an honorary visiting fellow for many years.